> *'O my friends be warned by me,*
> *That breakfast, dinner, lunch and tea*
> *Are all the human frame requires.'*
>
> Hilaire Belloc, *Cautionary Tales.*

The Farmer's Wife Cook Book is a cook book with a most interesting and important difference. All the recipes have been written by farmers' wives, and selected from over 1000 recipes sent in from all over the country, specially for this promotion.

The excellent recipes came almost literally from John O'Groats to Land's End, and from just about every type of farm and farming land in the country.

We judges based our selection on recipes that produced original, practical and delicious dishes, which were also economical and not too difficult to make.

I was one of the judges of this competition and it was a very difficult task to test so many excellent recipes and to select the winners.

Farm cooking in this country has always been exceptionally good, possibly for two main reasons: first, farmers' wives are usually very busy people; they have little time for shopping, so make use of the ingredients readily available; they need skill and creative ability to turn them into unusual and appetizing meals; secondly, British farmers' wives have access to some of the best *natural* produce in the world — high quality milk, cream, eggs, poultry, bacon etc.,— so their meals are nourishing as well as interesting.

Although the recipes were developed by country-women, they are equally suitable for those of us who live in towns and cities. Farmer's Wife produce is natural, and comes to us straight from the country; it is delivered direct to you by the milkman; so, with little time and effort *everyone* can cook these recipes.

I am sure this book will be of value to you and you will enjoy using it.

Breakfasts. Every farmer's wife knows just what a critical period breakfast time is. Rising before dawn every day, the farmer needs a substantial breakfast to protect him from the cold through a day's work.

The English breakfast is really world famous. Few countries have such a nourishing and warming way to start the day, but then few countries have a climate quite like ours. Our rich harvest of natural farm produce offers us a wide range of breakfast dishes to choose from. The bread, butter, milk, honeys, jams, bacon and eggs available in this country mean that we rarely have to look abroad for breakfast ideas. And with such a wide choice of dishes to tempt him, it's quite surprising that the farmer ever finds time to get out to the fields.

The winning recipe was submitted by Mrs. G. Leonard of Thetford. Her Farmhouse Pancakes were chosen for one simple reason—they taste marvellous. At the same time, they're quick and easy to make, and they are very nourishing.

Alternatively, you might like to try Welsh Farm Breakfast, a tangy melange of yogurt, cereal and fresh fruit that really wakes up the taste buds. An interesting combination of dishes that will make a change from bacon and eggs or toast and marmalade, is Honeyed Oats with Herring Roe Surprise to follow.

Try all the recipes, you'll find them all rewarding and satisfying, and you'll probably be able to make your own variations. It's really worth making the effort to produce a good breakfast every morning; it can put the whole family in a good mood for the rest of the day.

Mrs. M. Thomas, Wolverton Manor Farm, Stratford-on-Avon. Middle right
Mrs. S. Jerrard, The Wollands, Cockburnspath, Scotland. Bottom
Mrs. N. G. Gradidge, Knightwood Farm, Southampton, Hants. Middle left
Mrs. G. Leonard, Hall Farm, Thetford, Norfolk. Top

Farmhouse pancakes (*left*)

Mrs. G. Leonard, Hall Farm,
Thetford, Norfolk

3 rashers bacon, finely chopped
1 small onion, finely chopped
1 oz. fat for frying

Batter
4 oz. plain flour
seasoning
2 eggs
¼ pint milk
4 oz. sausage meat

Makes 6–8 pancakes

Fry the bacon and onion together in a small pan with a quarter of the fat, until the onion is soft and transparent. (If the bacon and onion are *very* finely chopped there is no need to fry them first.) Meanwhile make the batter. Sieve the flour and seasoning into a bowl and make a well in the centre. Break the eggs into it and beat them, gradually taking in the flour from the sides of the bowl. As the mixture thickens, add half the milk. When all the flour is incorporated, add the rest of the milk and beat well. Add the sausage meat to the batter, breaking it up with a fork and beating it in. Add the cooked bacon and onion and mix well. Heat the remaining fat in a frying pan and drop in 2 tablespoonfuls of the mixture for each pancake. Cook the pancakes until they are golden brown on each side, about 5 minutes. Serve with fried mushrooms and tomatoes.

Worcester sausage breakfast

Mrs. M. Thomas, Wolverton Manor Farm,
Stratford-on-Avon

1 lb. sausages
1 lb. cooking apples
1 tablespoon brown sugar
(*optional*)
¼ teaspoon cinnamon
chopped parsley to garnish

Serves 4

Cover the sausages with water, boil for 15 minutes. Peel, core and slice the apples. Drain most of the water from the sausages, leaving about 1 tablespoon in the pan. Add the sliced apples, sugar and the cinnamon and simmer gently for about 5 minutes, until the apple is soft. Garnish with chopped parsley.

Note If liked, the sausages can be grilled and added to the apples after they have been simmered in a little water.

Bedfordshire brochettes (*above*)

*Mrs. J. Labous, 1 Dimmock Road,
Wootton, Beds*

4 sausages
8 rashers bacon
8 button mushrooms
4 tomatoes
2 teaspoons cooking oil
seasoning
watercress to garnish

Serves 4

Divide the sausages into halves or quarters depending on their size. Roll up the bacon rashers. Brush the mushrooms and the halved tomatoes with a little cooking oil. Arrange the sausage, bacon, mushrooms and tomatoes, alternately on skewers and season. Grill for 10 minutes turning once or twice. Serve on the skewers. The sausages etc. are easily removed from the skewers by pushing from one end with a fork. Garnish with watercress.

Breakfast sausage slices

Miss H. Bailey, Lower Newnham Farm,
Broadwindsor, Beaminster

Hard-boil the eggs and cool under cold water. Remove
their shells. Grill the sausages. Meanwhile prepare
the cheese sauce. Melt the butter in a saucepan, add
the flour and cook for 1 minute over a low heat.
Remove the pan from the heat and gradually stir in
the milk. Return the pan to the heat and stir until the
sauce thickens and boils. Add most of the grated
cheese, saving a little for a topping. Add salt and
pepper and stir until the sauce becomes smooth.
Remove the pan from the heat but keep the sauce hot.
Toast and butter the slices of bread. Slice the grilled
sausages and arrange evenly on the toast. Slice the
eggs and arrange on top of the sausages. Pour cheese
sauce over each portion and top with the remaining
grated cheese. Grill for 2–3 minutes until brown.

2 large eggs
4 sausages

Cheese sauce
1 oz. butter
1 oz. flour
½ pint milk
2 oz. cheese, grated
¼ teaspoon salt
dash pepper
4 slices bread

Serves 4

Banff baconed bread

Mrs. H. R. Taylor, Upper Blairmaud Farm,
Boyndie, Banff

Remove the rind, with some of the fat, from the
bacon and set aside. Arrange 3 rashers on each slice of
bread and grill for 3–4 minutes. Slice the tomatoes
and mushrooms and arrange on top of the cooked
bacon. Place the bacon rinds on top to allow the fat,
as it melts, to run into the mushrooms and tomatoes
and return to the grill. Cook for 5 minutes until the
rinds become crispy. Remove the rinds and serve.

6 rashers bacon (with rind)
2 slices bread, buttered
2 tomatoes
4 mushrooms

Serves 2

Fluffy eggs

Mrs. M. Lyttle, Moss Side,
Portaferry, Co. Down

4 slices Cheddar cheese
$\frac{1}{2}$ teaspoon made mustard
4 slices cooked ham
4 eggs
seasoning
chopped parsley to garnish

Serves 4

Arrange the cheese slices in the base of a lightly greased shallow ovenproof dish. Spread with the mustard and cover with the ham slices. Bake in the centre of a preheated moderately hot oven (375°F, 190°C, Gas Mark 5) for 10 minutes. Separate the egg yolks from the whites. Beat and season the yolks and pour over the cheese and ham. Return to the oven for a further 5 minutes. Lower the temperature to moderate (325°F, 170°C, Gas Mark 3). Whisk the whites until stiff and spread over the cooked egg yolks. Return the dish to the oven and bake for a further 10–15 minutes. Garnish with chopped parsley before serving.

Cheesy potato scones

Mrs. G. E. Lowndes, Villa Farm,
Coton Clanford, Nr. Stafford

3 heaped tablespoons mashed potato
2 oz. cheese, grated
1 oz. butter
1 egg, beaten
2 oz. self-raising flour
1 oz. cooking fat for frying, or fat from fried bacon or sausages

Makes 6

Mix all the ingredients together to form a soft dough. Flour hands and divide the mixture into six rounds, shaping each lightly with the fingertips. Heat the fat until very hot and fry the scones quickly on each side to crisp and seal them. Lower the heat and continue to fry gently for about 5 minutes until cooked through. Drain on absorbent paper and serve with fried egg and bacon.

Herring roe surprise

Mrs. Grace Davies, Penyworlod Farm,
Erwood, Builth Wells, Breconshire

8 oz. soft herring roe
4 eggs
2 tablespoons chopped parsley
salt and pepper
fat for frying
toast or fried bread
juice of $\frac{1}{2}$ lemon

Makes 10–12

Break up the roe with a fork in a basin. Add the eggs to the roe and beat together well. Add the chopped parsley, salt and pepper. Heat a little fat in a frying pan and drop in 2 tablespoonfuls of mixture, spreading it thinly round the pan. Brown lightly, turn, and brown the other side. Serve hot, on toast or fried bread, with a squeeze of lemon juice.

Sunshine starter (*above*)

Mrs. S. M. Jerrard, The Woollands,
By Cockburnspath, Berwickshire

Poach fish gently in the milk until cooked, about
5 minutes. Remove the fish and flake; keep it warm.
Toast the bread and spread with half the butter.
Divide the rest of the butter between two cups of an
egg poacher and break an egg into each. When cooked,
place each egg on a slice of toast and surround with
the flaked fish. Season with salt and pepper and
garnish with chopped parsley or paprika pepper.

1 medium finnan haddock fillet
¼ pint milk
2 slices bread
1 oz. butter
2 eggs
salt and pepper
chopped parsley to garnish

Serves 2

Welsh farm breakfast (*above*)

Mrs. D. Crooks, Parcmawr,
Talley, Llandeilo

¼ *pint natural yogurt or* ½ *pint milk*
juice of ½ *lemon*
2 tablespoons clear honey or syrup
8 tablespoons porridge oats
3 tablespoons chopped nuts
2 tablespoons raisins or sultanas
1 large red-skinned apple, cored and
chopped
apple slices, dipped in lemon juice

Serves 2

Combine the yogurt or milk, lemon juice and honey.
Add the remaining ingredients and mix thoroughly.
Allow to stand for 30 minutes before serving.
Decorate with apple slices.

Note This can be made and left to stand overnight,
but do not add the apple until serving, as it tends to
go brown.
If liked, other fruit can be used in place
of the apple.

Honeyed oats

Mrs. R. Dutton, Upton Grange, Upton-by-Chester

Mix the oats, flakes and sultanas in a cereal bowl.
Trail the honey from a spoon all over the mixture.
Beat the egg and milk together and when ready to eat
pour onto the dish.

Note If you do not want to cook breakfast, are tired of
cornflakes and toast and would prefer to go to work
on an egg, this is both delicious and very sustaining.
Raisins or currants can be used in place of the sultanas.

2 tablespoons porridge oats
*3 tablespoons bran or wheat
flakes*
2 teaspoons sultanas
1 teaspoon clear honey
1 egg
about ¼ pint milk

Serves 1

Nutty yogurt

*Mrs. M. Hull, Turncole Farm,
Southminster, Essex*

Place the yogurt, apple, banana, orange or tangerine,
orange juice, nibbed almonds and hazelnuts in a bowl.
Mix all the ingredients together with a wooden
spoon. Spoon the mixture into individual serving
dishes to serve. If liked, the nutty yogurt can be
decorated with extra slices of fruit, or some of the
prepared fruit can be kept aside and used for
decoration. Any selection of fruit, fresh or canned,
can be used.

2 5-oz. cartons natural yogurt
1 dessert apple, thinly sliced
1 banana, sliced
½ orange or tangerine, sliced
2 teaspoons orange juice
1 oz. nibbed almonds
1 oz. hazelnuts, chopped

Serves 2

Quick farm rolls

*Mrs. N. L. Gradidge, Knightwood Farm,
Southampton*

Sieve the flour, salt and baking powder into a bowl.
Rub in the butter. Beat the egg and add most of it to
the milk, reserving a little for glazing the rolls. Add
the egg and milk to the flour and bind the mixture
together. Without kneading, quickly divide and shape
the dough into 16 even pieces. Place on a greased
baking tray and brush with the remaining egg. Bake
in the centre of a preheated hot oven (425°F, 220°C,
Gas Mark 7) for 12–15 minutes. Serve hot with butter.

1 lb. plain flour
1 teaspoon salt
2 teaspoons baking powder
2 oz. butter
1 egg
½ pint milk

Makes 16

*'First they brought pâtés, then they brought fish.
The first course was herald to a tasty main dish.'*

Old English Ballad.

Starters.
The first course of any meal is the one that makes or breaks it. Deciding what to serve is as much an art as preparing and cooking it properly.

The starter's main job is to liven up the palate for the main course, so it has to be a really piquant dish. But it should also complement the main course—there should be a balance between the tastes, the textures and the colours.

Salmacado was chosen as the winner in this section because it represented everything that a starter should be. First it's delicious, the rich taste of the salmon sets off the blandness of the avocado flesh perfectly. Then it's light, it won't fill you up and put you off the main course. Next it's not difficult to prepare, and this can be done in advance, leaving you to put the finishing touch to the main course, or entertain your guests. Finally it looks attractive and appetizing just sitting on the table waiting to be eaten. Salmacado would be an excellent starter to any of the main meals in this book, but it would go particularly well before the Pheasant in Red Wine, the Spicy Chicken or the Pigeon and Giblet Pie.

Baked Stuffed Mackerel was also one of the favourites; it could be served before a light main course dish.

When choosing a starter, bear in mind how it is to be served. If it's to be a buffet meal, choose a dish that is easy to eat standing up—Chicken Nuggets for instance, or the Smoked Haddock Pâté, which could be served on fingers of brown toast or slices of pumpernickel.

Any starter will benefit from some garnish—it's useful to have some radishes, gherkins, chives, parsley and lemon to garnish with at the last moment.

Serve a light white wine with the first course. Any Riesling is usually a safe bet, and not too expensive. Chill it well, and together with your starter, your meal will be off to a flying start.

Mrs. E. Henman, Gate Farm Cottage, Kiddington, Oxon. Middle right
Mrs. L. Hodgson, Waterloo Farm, Sandy, Beds. Middle
Mrs. M. Hunter, Red Barn, Sherborne, Norfolk. Bottom
Mrs. S. Lawrence, Upper Aynho Grounds, Oxon. Top

Salmacado *(below)*

Mrs. Stephanie Lawrence, Upper Aynho Grounds, Aynho, Nr. Banbury

Flake the salmon and put on one side. Dissolve the gelatine in the hot water and put on one side. Mash the avocado flesh and add a good squeeze of lemon juice, salt and pepper to taste, mayonnaise, cream and dissolved gelatine. Mix all the ingredients together and turn into a lightly oiled 7-inch ring mould. Place in the refrigerator to set. When set, turn out and serve garnished with watercress and slices of cucumber.

1 7½-oz. can red salmon or
8 oz. fresh salmon, cooked
½ oz. gelatine
1 tablespoon hot water
2 ripe avocado pears
lemon juice
salt and pepper
3 tablespoons mayonnaise
4 tablespoons double cream
watercress and slices of
  cucumber to garnish

Serves 4

Smoked haddock pâté (below)

Mrs. L. Hodgson, Waterloo Farm,
Everton, Sandy, Beds

12 oz. smoked haddock
4 oz. butter, melted
1 7½-oz. carton double cream
2 teaspoons lemon juice
1 teaspoon Worcestershire
sauce
pepper and cayenne pepper
lemon fans and parsley
to garnish

Serves 6

Wipe the fish and poach in simmering water for 10 minutes. Drain, skin and flake finely. Allow to cool and mix with half the melted butter. Lightly whip the cream and fold in the fish mixture, lemon juice and Worcestershire sauce. Season to taste with the pepper and cayenne pepper. Spoon into a serving dish (or individual dishes) and leave to set. Cover the top of the pâté with the remaining melted butter and leave to set again. Serve garnished with lemon fans and parsley.

Cheese scampi

Mrs. M. J. Parrott, Beech Farm,
Trentham, Stoke-on-Trent

6 rashers streaky bacon
4 oz. frozen scampi

Cheese sauce
½ oz. butter
½ oz. flour
¼ pint milk
4 oz. Cheddar cheese, grated

Serves 4

Cut the rinds off the bacon rashers and put them in a hot oven (425°F, 220°C, Gas Mark 7) for 15 minutes. When crisp, chop the rinds and set aside. Cut the bacon rashers in half and wrap each piece around a frozen scampi. Place on a baking tray and cook for 12–15 minutes at the top of the hot oven. Meanwhile prepare the cheese sauce. Melt the butter in a saucepan, add the flour and cook for 1 minute over a low heat. Remove the pan from the heat and stir in the milk; cook, stirring, until the sauce is smooth and creamy. Add the cheese and stir until melted. Pour over the bacon and scampi rolls and sprinkle with the chopped crisp bacon rinds.

Sea cream starter

Mrs. Daphne Olley, West Cottage,
Flimwell, Wadhurst, Sussex

Mix the cheese, cream and shallot or garlic together until smooth. Whip the egg white until stiff and fold into the cream cheese mixture. Gently fold in the caviar (reserving a little to garnish) or fish (if using haddock or kipper fillets pound or liquidise them with the egg yolk); season to taste. Spoon into individual dishes and garnish with the reserved caviar and parsley. Serve with toast.

4 oz. cream cheese
2 tablespoons single cream
1 small shallot or sliver garlic,
crushed
1 egg white
1 3½-oz. jar mock caviar or 4 oz.
cooked smoked haddock or kipper
fillets
seasoning

Serves 4

Baked stuffed mackerel *(below)*

Mrs. Vivien Midgley, 23 Elmtrees,
Long Crendon, Aylesbury

Melt the butter and fry the onion until softened. Add the chopped apple, breadcrumbs, herbs, lemon rind and juice and seasoning. Open each fish out flat and press out the backbone. Divide the stuffing between them. Roll up, from the wide end, and secure each with a wooden cocktail stick. Place in an ovenproof dish, brush with oil and cover with foil or a lid. Bake in the centre of a preheated moderate oven (350°F, 180 C, Gas Mark 4) for 30 minutes. Arrange on a serving dish, garnish with lemon slices and parsley and serve with thinly sliced brown bread and butter.

1 oz. butter
1 onion, chopped
1 apple, chopped
3 oz. fresh white breadcrumbs
½ teaspoon mixed herbs
grated rind and juice of ½ lemon
salt and pepper
4 medium mackerel, cleaned
oil for brushing
lemon slices and
parsley to garnish

Serves 4

Sweetcorn-stuffed tomatoes (*below*)

*Mrs. Barbara Hendry, Auchinhove Farm,
Keith, Banff*

Halve the tomatoes, scoop out the centres and mix
with the cream cheese, cream and sweetcorn. Season
to taste and spoon back into the tomato cases.
Arrange on a bed of lettuce leaves and serve
garnished with parsley.

Variation Hard-boiled eggs can be used instead of,
or as well as, tomatoes.

6 large tomatoes
2 oz. cream cheese
2 tablespoons single cream
4 oz. cooked frozen or fresh
sweetcorn, or canned
seasoning
1 lettuce
parsley to garnish

Serves 6

Avocado soufflé

*Mrs. M. Hunter, Red Barn,
Sherborne, Kings Lynn*

Melt the butter, add the flour and cook together for
1 minute, stirring. Off the heat, gradually add the
milk. Stir over the heat until the sauce thickens. Cool
slightly, then beat in the egg yolks, seasoning, lemon
juice and avocado flesh – do not reheat. Whisk the
egg whites until stiff and fold into the avocado
mixture. Turn into an 8-inch soufflé dish and cook in
the centre of a preheated moderate oven (350°F,
180°C, Gas Mark 4) for 45 minutes. Serve at once.

$1\frac{1}{2}$ oz. butter
$1\frac{1}{2}$ oz. flour
$\frac{1}{4}$ pint milk
4 eggs
salt and pepper
2 teaspoons lemon juice
flesh of 2 just-ripe avocado
pears, chopped

Serves 4

Asparagus mousse

Mrs. Elizabeth Henman, Gate Farm Cottage,
Kiddington, Oxon

Dissolve the gelatine in the boiling water. Mix together the cream, yogurt, egg yolks, lemon juice and seasoning. Stir in the cooled gelatine. Drain and chop the asparagus tips (reserve 6 asparagus tops to garnish). As the mixture begins to thicken fold in the chopped asparagus and whipped egg whites. Spoon into six ramekin dishes and leave to set. Garnish with the reserved asparagus tops, small lemon fans and paprika pepper.

½ oz. gelatine
2 tablespoons boiling water
¼ pint single cream
1 5-oz. carton natural yogurt
2 eggs, separated
2 teaspoons lemon juice
salt, pepper and paprika pepper
1 10-oz. can asparagus tips
lemon fans and paprika pepper to garnish

Serves 6

Chicken and herb refresher *(below)*

Mrs. R. Hazlerigg, Cottonsfield Farm,
Billesdon, Leicester

Mix all the ingredients together and put in the refrigerator for 2 hours or more. Serve in individual bowls and garnish with lemon slices and chives.

2 5-oz. cartons natural yogurt
½ pint milk
¼ cucumber, chopped
4 oz. pickled gherkins, chopped
4 oz. cooked chicken, chopped
little chopped fennel, mint, chives
and parsley
seasoning
lemon slices and chives to garnish

Serves 4

Summer soup

*Mrs. Caroline Kendon, Quedley Farm,
Flimwell, Wadhurst, Sussex*

*1 oz. butter
1 medium onion, peeled and chopped
1 1-lb. 12-oz. can tomato soup
½ cucumber
2 drops Tabasco sauce or pinch
cayenne pepper
seasoning
4 tablespoons single cream
chopped parsley to garnish*

Serves 4

Heat the butter and fry the onion gently until
softened. Drain off any excess butter. Add the soup
together with the diced cucumber, Tabasco sauce or
cayenne pepper and seasoning. Bring slowly to just
below boiling point. Spoon into heated soup bowls
and top each with 1 tablespoonful of cream. Sprinkle
with chopped parsley and serve croûtons separately.

Farmhouse onion soup (*above*)

Mrs. Hardie, Newfarm, Errol, Perthshire

Peel and slice the onions thinly. Heat the butter in a
large saucepan, add a little sugar and the onions and
cook them very gently, over a low heat, stirring
constantly until the rings are an even golden brown.
Gradually add the beef stock stirring all the time.
Bring the soup to the boil, lower the heat, cover and
simmer gently for 1 hour. Just before serving stir the
brandy (if used) into the soup and add salt and
pepper. Toast the slices of French bread lightly on
each side, cover one side with grated Gruyère cheese
and brown under the grill (or brown in the oven). To
serve, float the rounds of toast and cheese in the bowl
of soup. Garnish with parsley.

*2–3 large onions
2 oz. butter
little sugar
2½ pints beef stock
scant ¼ pint brandy (optional)
salt
freshly ground black pepper
4–6 slices French bread
grated Gruyere cheese
parsley to garnish*

Serves 4–6

Savoury cheese pears (*below left*)

Mrs. Phyllis Brown, Downside,
Silver Street Lane, Trowbridge

Peel the pears, slice in half and remove the cores.
Dip the pear halves in lemon juice to prevent them
discolouring. Mix together the cream cheese,
mayonnaise and cream. Add seasoning and fold in
the parsley and bacon. Divide the mixture between
the pear halves and arrange, on a bed of lettuce or
watercress, on a serving dish.
Garnish with bacon rolls.

4 ripe pears
lemon juice
4 oz. cream cheese
4 teaspoons mayonnaise
4 tablespoons double cream
salt and pepper
4 teaspoons chopped parsley
4 oz. cooked bacon, finely chopped
lettuce or watercress
bacon rolls to garnish

Serves 4

Grapefruit surprise (*below right*)

Mrs. D. Leggett, Langrick, Boston, Lincs

Halve the grapefruit, remove and chop the segments
and mix with the yogurt, half the sugar and the
brandy (if used). Remove the membranes and any
pips from the grapefruit halves. Spoon the fruit and
yogurt mixture back into the grapefruit halves.
Sprinkle with the remaining sugar and place
under a preheated grill to melt the sugar.
Decorate with a glacé cherry and serve
immediately.

Note If liked, omit the glacé cherries
and decorate with chopped nuts.

2 grapefruit
1 5-oz. carton natural yogurt
2 tablespoons brown sugar
2 tablespoons brandy (optional)
4 glacé cherries

Serves 4

Liver and anchovy pâté (*below*)

Mrs. D. Chick, Manor Farm,
Handley, Nr. Salisbury, Wilts

Mince the liver, fat bacon and garlic twice; place in a mixing bowl. Mince the anchovies and place with the liver mixture. Place the milk, onion, peppercorns, one of the bay leaves, the mace and seasoning in a pan. Bring slowly to the boil, then strain. Melt the butter in the pan. Add the flour and cook, stirring, for 1–2 minutes. Gradually add the flavoured milk, stirring all the time. Bring to the boil and cook until thickened. Combine the sauce with the ingredients in the mixing bowl. Place the remaining bay leaves in the base of a 2-lb. loaf tin and line the tin with the streaky bacon rashers. Spoon in the liver mixture. Stand the tin in a pan of water and cook in the centre of a preheated moderate oven (350°F, 180°C, Gas Mark 4) for 1 hour. Remove from the oven, place a weight on top of the pâté and leave in the refrigerator for 2 days. Turn onto a serving dish and serve with hot toast.

12 oz. pig's liver
4 oz. fat bacon
1 clove garlic
1 can anchovies
½ pint milk
1 slice onion
4 peppercorns
3 bay leaves

½ teaspoon ground mace
salt and pepper
1 oz. butter
¾ oz. flour
4 oz. streaky bacon rashers

Serves 6–8

Chicken nuggets and dip (*below*)

Mrs. M. Hewson, White House,
Thornby, Wigton, Cumberland

Make the nuggets by combining all the ingredients in a bowl and mixing well. Form the mixture into balls using about 2 teaspoonfuls for each. Heat the butter and oil in a frying pan and add the meatballs. Turning frequently, cook them gently for 10 minutes. Drain and serve, hot or cold on cocktail sticks, with the dip made by combining all the ingredients in a bowl and seasoning to taste. Garnish with parsley.

Note These would be suitable to serve as a party dip. The nuggets can be varied by omitting the bacon and chicken and substituting cooked minced pork. If liked a dash of Tabasco or Worcestershire sauce can be added.

Nuggets
4 oz. lean bacon, minced
4 oz. uncooked chicken, minced
2 oz. spring onions,
finely chopped
1 5-oz. can water chestnuts,
drained and finely chopped
1 egg, beaten
1 clove garlic, crushed
(optional)
salt and pepper
1 oz. butter and 2 tablespoons
cooking oil for frying

Dip
1 5-oz. carton natural yogurt
4 oz. cottage cheese
1 8-oz. can crushed pineapple,
drained
1 tablespoon finely chopped onion
1 tablespoon finely chopped parsley
seasoning
parsley to garnish

Serves 4–5

Celery savoury starters (*below*)

*Mrs. Eileen Richardson, Barn Farm,
Aston-by-Doxry, Stafford*

Make the egg filling by hard-boiling the eggs and
cooling under cold water. When cold, shell and chop
or mash together with the mayonnaise. Make the
cream cheese and chive filling by mixing the cheese
and chives in a bowl, using the milk to moisten. Make
the cream cheese and pineapple filling in the same
way. Cut the celery sticks into 2½-inch lengths. Fill
one-third of the sticks with egg filling, and garnish
with mustard and cress. Fill another third with
cream cheese and chives, and garnish with parsley.
Fill the remaining third with cream cheese and
pineapple and garnish with pineapple. Arrange the
filled celery sticks decoratively on a serving tray,
or if available a slice of fresh pineapple.

*1 head celery, split into sticks,
washed and trimmed*

Egg filling
*3 eggs
2 tablespoons mayonnaise
    mustard and cress to garnish*

Cream cheese and chive filling
*4 oz. cream cheese with chives or
plain cream cheese mixed with
1 tablespoon chopped chives
1 tablespoon milk to moisten
    parsley to garnish*

Cream cheese and pineapple filling
*4 oz. cream cheese with pineapple or
plain cream cheese mixed with
2 tablespoons drained crushed
pineapple
1 tablespoon milk to moisten
pineapple to garnish*

Serves 6

'His hound is to the hunting gone,
His hawk to fetch the wild fowl home.
His lady's ta'en another mate,
So we may make our dinner sweet.'

Scottish Ballad.

Main meals.
In this country, we have the chance to taste some of the finest food in the world. Our farmers can supply almost any food that the world has to offer, and generally supply it better. If cooked properly, we think that none of these dishes could be improved upon anywhere else in the world.

All the recipes depend on is care in preparation, and honest, country fresh foodstuffs. They all make use of the type of food that people in this country have been eating for hundreds of years: game, fowl, fish, pork, beef, mutton, fresh fruit and vegetables, and home-grown herbs. The winning recipe in this section comes from Mrs. J. Whitfield of Market Deeping. Her Pheasant in Red Wine owes a little of its taste to the skills of the French winemaker; nevertheless, it is a dish that has been eaten in this country for centuries. Remember, when you are choosing a pheasant, that a cock bird will usually feed four people, whereas a hen bird will generally only feed two.

Pheasant is at its best in October and November when it should not be too difficult to obtain.

If you cook the Highland Fare recipe, let the venison hang for a couple of days beforehand to improve the flavour. The venison recipe comes from Mrs. F. Gunn of Caithness. Obviously, Mrs. Gunn has more access to local game than most of us, but you may be surprised to find that venison is easy to get hold of in most parts of the country, and not too expensive.

Mrs. N. J. Woollacott's Pigeon and Giblet Pie is an economical dish that makes use of foods that are easy to buy anywhere.

Beef and Cider Casserole, a Yorkshire dish, was another favourite with the judges. It's a dish that can be prepared in advance, and can be left in a low oven for several hours. Last but not least, do try the Croft Fish Casserole. It's the only fish dish in the section, but don't snub the poor old fish just because it's not grown on the land.

Mrs. J. Whitfield, Gibbs Farm, Peterborough. Top
Mrs. M. Blacker, White House Farm, Newton-on-Ouse, Yorks. Middle right
Mrs. H. Aitkin, Red Farm, Yarm-on-Tees, Yorks. Bottom
Mrs. M. Parry, Llanborth Farm, Llandysul, Wales. Middle left

Pheasant in red wine (*left*)

Mrs. J. Whitfield, Gibbs Farm, Meadows Road,
Market Deeping, Peterborough

2 small pheasants
3 oz. butter
4 oz. button mushrooms
8 oz. button onions
$\frac{1}{2}$ oz. flour
$\frac{1}{4}$ pint red wine
$\frac{1}{4}$ pint chicken stock
1 tablespoon soft brown sugar

Stuffing
1 large cooking apple, grated
1 stick celery, grated
1 oz. butter, melted
1 oz. sultanas
grated rind and juice of $\frac{1}{2}$ lemon
salt and pepper
1 oz. fresh white breadcrumbs
watercress and fried apple rings
to garnish

Serves 4–6

Clean the pheasants. To make the stuffing place the grated apple and celery in a bowl. Mix in the melted butter, the sultanas, lemon rind and juice, seasoning and breadcrumbs. Use to stuff the birds; truss them if necessary. Melt the butter in a large, thick-based frying pan and quickly brown the pheasants all over. Place in a large casserole dish. Add the mushrooms and onions to the frying pan and sauté for 2–3 minutes. Place around the pheasants in the casserole dish. Stir in the flour to the butter remaining in the pan; gradually add wine and stock; stirring, bring to the boil. Add the sugar and boil the liquid until it has reduced by one-third. Pour into the casserole dish, cover and cook in the centre of a preheated moderate oven (350°F, 180°C, Gas Mark 4) for about 1 hour – baste the pheasants during cooking with the liquor. Serve from the casserole dish or arrange the pheasants on a serving dish and surround with the sauce, mushrooms and onions. Garnish with watercress and apple rings; serve with game chips and baby carrots and courgettes, or with a green salad.

Highland fare

Mrs. F. Gunn, Watten Mains,
Watten, Caithness

2 lb. venison
1 oz. dripping
2 onions, sliced
4 oz. bacon, chopped
8 oz. cranberries
8 oz. chestnuts, peeled
2 teaspoons salt
$\frac{1}{2}$ teaspoon pepper
about $\frac{1}{4}$ pint port
1$\frac{1}{2}$ pints stock
1 oz. butter
1 oz. flour
2 tablespoons single cream

Serves 6

Cut the venison into 1-inch pieces. Melt the dripping in a flameproof casserole and brown the meat pieces on all sides. Add the onions and bacon and sauté for 2–3 minutes. Stir in the cranberries, chestnuts, seasoning, port and stock. Cover and cook in the centre of a preheated moderate oven (350°F, 180°C, Gas Mark 4) for about 1$\frac{1}{2}$ hours, until the meat is tender. Blend the butter and flour together and whisk small pieces of it into the casserole and cook for a further 20 minutes. Just before serving, pour over the cream. Serve with boiled potatoes and celery.

Pigeon and giblet pie (*left*)

*Mrs. N.J. Woollacott, 'Capitol', Bishops,
South Molton, Devon*

4–5 pigeons
1 medium onion stuck with
6–8 cloves
duck or chicken giblets
1 oz. butter
6-8 oz. bacon, diced
1 pig's or lamb's kidney
1 tablespoon flour
¼ pint single cream
1 large egg
salt and pepper
pinch ground mace
8 oz. puff or flaky pastry
beaten egg to glaze

Serves 6

Put the cleaned and prepared pigeons in a pan
with the onion and cover with fresh cold water.
Bring to the boil, cover and simmer until tender. Put
the giblets in a separate pan, cover with water and
simmer until tender. Melt the butter in a pan and fry
the bacon for 2–3 minutes. Remove and add the diced
kidney and cook for 4 minutes. When the pigeons
are cooked, take the meat off the bones and place in an
8-inch pie dish with the cooked bacon and kidney.
Blend the flour into the fat remaining in the
frying pan and cook, stirring for 1 minute. Whisk the
cream and egg together and add sufficient stock to
make enough liquid to almost fill the dish. Blend into
the flour and, stirring, cook until thickened – do not
boil. Add seasoning to taste and pour into the pie
dish. Leave to cool. Roll out the pastry to a round a
little larger than the pie, cut off a strip and place on
the edge of the pie dish. Dampen the pastry strip and
cover the pie with the remaining pastry. Flake and
flute the edges. Make a hole in the centre and make a
decoration from any pastry trimmings. Brush with
beaten egg and bake in the centre of a preheated
moderately hot oven (400°F, 200°C, Gas Mark 6) for
25–30 minutes. Serve hot with creamed potatoes,
green peas or carrots, and gravy.

Harvest casserole

*Mrs. D. Randall, Slade Farm,
Hedgerley, Slough*

4–6 pigeons
seasoning
6 shallots or small onions
4 oz. button mushrooms
8 oz. small whole carrots
4 rashers streaky bacon, diced
¼ pint red wine or port
1 tablespoon cornflour

Serves 4–6

Cover the pigeons with water, season and simmer
gently until the breast meat can easily be removed,
about 1½ hours. Retain about 1 pint of the stock.
Place the meat in a casserole, add the vegetables,
bacon and wine. Blend the cornflour with a little
strained pigeon stock and pour, with the rest of the
stock, over the casserole. Season and cook in a preheated moderate oven (350°F, 180°C, Gas Mark 4)
for about 1½ hours, until the vegetables are cooked.

Orchard chicken

Mrs. Ann Taylor, Mosswood Farm,
Shotley Bridge, Co. Durham

Prepare the stuffing by combining all the dry ingredients with the beaten egg. Stuff the chicken, truss it and put in a roasting pan. Pour the wine, apple juice and stock around the base of the chicken, cover with foil and cook in a preheated moderate oven (350°F, 180°C, Gas Mark 4). After 1 hour remove the foil and allow the chicken to brown for remaining cooking time, about 30 minutes. When cooked put the chicken on a serving dish and keep hot. Blend the cornflour with a little water and add to the juice in the roasting pan. Bring to the boil stirring all the time as it thickens. Serve in a gravy boat. The chicken should be garnished with apple rings fried in a little butter and bacon rolls made from half a rasher, rolled and baked in the oven for 10 minutes. Tuck a sprig of parsley between the drumsticks.

1 roasting chicken, 3–3½ lb.
¼ pint white wine
½ pint apple juice
¼ pint chicken stock
½ oz. cornflour

Stuffing
5 oz. fresh white breadcrumbs
½ cooking apple, grated
1 small onion, finely chopped
3 oz. streaky bacon, chopped
1 teaspoon dried tarragon
salt and pepper
1 egg, beaten

Garnish
2 apples, cored and cut into ¼-inch
rings
butter
4 bacon rashers
parsley

Serves 4–5

Farmhouse chicken

Mrs. Margaret Parry, Llanborth Farm,
Llandysul, Cardiganshire

Melt half the butter in a frying pan and fry the chicken joints quickly, browning on both sides. Remove the joints from the pan and place in a casserole. Add the remaining butter to the frying pan and fry the shallots and mushrooms for 2–3 minutes, then put them in the casserole on top of the chicken joints. Add the flour to the fat remaining in the frying pan and mix to a smooth paste, cooking over a gentle heat. Take the frying pan off the heat and gradually blend in the wine, stock, Tabasco sauce and cream. Return the pan to the heat and bring the sauce just to the boil, stirring all the time. Pour the sauce over the contents of the casserole, cover and cook in the centre of a moderate oven (350°F, 180°C, Gas Mark 4) for 1–1½ hours. Serve garnished with chopped parsley.

2 oz. butter
4 chicken joints
8 shallots
8 oz. button mushrooms
1 tablespoon flour
¼ pint white wine
½ pint chicken stock
½ teaspoon Tabasco sauce
3 tablespoons cream
seasoning
chopped parsley to garnish

Serves 4

Eastern shepherd's pie

Miss M. L. Miles, 9 Fabricius Avenue, Droitwich

1 oz. butter
1 large onion, finely chopped
1 teaspoon flour
2 tablespoons curry powder
1 8-oz. can tomatoes
2 tablespoons tomato purée
$\frac{1}{2}$ pint chicken stock
1 teaspoon salt
1 teaspoon sugar
juice of $\frac{1}{2}$ lemon
2 tablespoons chutney
12 oz.–1 lb. cooked chicken or
turkey, chopped
1 cooking apple, chopped
2 tablespoons cream
1 lb. mashed potatoes

Serves 3–4

Melt the butter in a large saucepan and fry the chopped onion until golden brown. Stir in the flour and curry powder and cook for 2 minutes. Stir in the tomatoes, tomato purée and half the stock. Add the salt, sugar, lemon juice and chutney and simmer for 30 minutes, stirring occasionally. Add the chicken, chopped apple and the rest of the stock. Simmer a further 15–20 minutes, stirring occasionally. Stir in the cream and transfer the mixture to a deep oven-proof dish. Cover with mashed potato and brown under the grill. Serve garnished with parsley.

Note Cooked minced beef or lamb can be used in place of the chicken or turkey, in which case omit the lemon juice and cream and use beef stock instead of the chicken stock. If liked, the dish can be garnished with tomato slices.

Spicy chicken

Mrs. S. R. Torrens, Lower Mill Cottage, Furnace Lane, Madeley, Nr. Crewe

1 roasting chicken, about 3$\frac{1}{2}$ lb.
$\frac{3}{4}$ pint strong chicken stock
2 oz. butter
3 large onions, sliced
$\frac{1}{2}$ pint boiling water
3 tablespoons tomato purée
3 teaspoons ground ginger
2 tablespoons soft brown sugar
8 oz. long-grain rice
$\frac{1}{4}$ pint double cream (optional)
1 oz. almonds, blanched
and chopped

Serves 4

Place the chicken, in an uncovered roasting tin, in the centre of a moderate oven (350°F, 180°C, Gas Mark 4). After 45 minutes–1 hour, when the skin is crisp and starting to brown, pour the stock around the base of the chicken and return the pan to the oven. Melt the butter in a frying pan and cook the sliced onions gently until soft and transparent. Add the boiling water to the frying pan and stir in the tomato purée. Bring to the boil again and add the ground ginger and soft brown sugar. Stir the spicy sauce mixture into the stock around the chicken and return the roasting pan to the oven until the chicken is completely cooked – 20–30 minutes depending on the weight of the bird. Meanwhile cook the rice in boiling salted water for 12 minutes, drain and rinse with boiling water. Fork over and place at the bottom of the oven to dry. Arrange the rice on a large dish and place the jointed chicken on top. Spoon the spicy sauce over. Pour on the cream (if used) and sprinkle with the chopped almonds.

Farmers' favourite

Mrs. F. Such, Maer Heath,
Baldwins Gate, Stoke-on-Trent

Melt the butter in a shallow flameproof dish. Fry the sliced onions. Halve the kidneys and remove the cores. Fry with the onions. Mix the wine, ketchup and Worcestershire sauce and pour into the pan. Season, cover and simmer for 30 minutes. Just before serving add the chopped parsley and pour on the cream. Serve when hot, but do not allow to boil.

Note When cooking kidneys it is important not to cook them for too long as they will become hard. Calves' kidneys can be used instead of lambs'.

2 oz. butter
2 onions, sliced
8 lambs' kidneys
¼ pint white wine
2 tablespoons mushroom ketchup
2 tablespoons Worcestershire sauce
seasoning
2 tablespoons chopped parsley
¼ pint single cream

Serves 4

34

Dairy meatballs (*left*)

Mrs. Beckett, Middle Traine, Brownston Street, Modbury, Devon

Meatballs
1 lb. minced beef
1 egg, beaten
½ oz. butter
1 onion, finely chopped
1 clove garlic, chopped and crushed with salt
1 tablespoon tomato purée
1 teaspoon dried thyme
¼ teaspoon pepper
little flour

Sauce
2 meat stock cubes
1 pint water
1 onion, chopped
1 bay leaf
seasoning
1 tablespoon cornflour
1 5-oz. carton natural yogurt or ¼ pint soured cream
chopped parsley and triangles of toast to garnish

Serves 4

Make the stock for the sauce by simmering the stock cubes in the water together with the chopped onion, bay leaf and seasoning for 10 minutes. Remove from the heat and leave to infuse. To prepare the meatballs, put the minced beef in a basin and add the beaten egg. Melt the butter, fry the chopped onion until soft then add it to the meat mixture. Add the garlic, tomato purée, thyme and pepper. Bind all the ingredients together. Flour the hands and shape the meat mixture into balls, about the size of a walnut. Strain the stock into another pan, bring to the boil and drop in the meatballs to cook for 30 minutes. Remove the meatballs and pile onto a serving dish. Keep hot. Blend the cornflour with a little water add it to the stock, heat and stir until the sauce thickens. Add the yogurt or soured cream and when hot, but not boiling, pour sauce over the meatballs. Garnish with chopped parsley and triangles of toast.

Variations Use sausage meat instead of minced beef, or substitute mace or nutmeg for thyme, or enrich the sauce by adding a few cooked slices of mushroom and green pepper.

Beef and cider casserole

Mrs. Hazel Aitkin, Red Hall Farm, Castle Levington, Yarm-on-Tees, Yorks

2 oz. butter
1 small onion, chopped
3 oz. bacon, chopped
2 oz. mushrooms, chopped
2 carrots, chopped
1½ lb. stewing steak
2 tablespoons flour
½ pint beef stock
½ pint cider
seasoning

Serves 5–6

Melt the butter in a frying pan and fry the onion, bacon, mushrooms and carrots for 5 minutes. Drain and place in the bottom of a casserole. Divide the meat into 5 or 6 portions, coat with a little flour and fry until browned. Place on top of the vegetables in the casserole. Blend the rest of the flour with the butter in the frying pan and cook until it browns. Remove from the heat and gradually stir in the beef stock. Bring to the boil over the heat stirring well. Pour over the casserole. Add the cider and cook in a preheated cool oven (275°F, 140°C, Gas Mark 1) for 2–2½ hours.

Yorkshire bacon (*above*)

Mrs. M. A. Blacker, White House Farm,
Newton-on-Ouse, Yorks

Cut the bacon into bite-sized pieces. Melt the butter in a frying pan and fry the bacon and sliced onion together for 5 minutes. Put into a casserole. Remove the seeds from the pepper and cut into thin strips; add to the casserole. Drain the apricots and make the juice up to ½ pint with water. Blend a little with the cornflour in a pan then add the rest of the juice. Add the vinegar and soy sauce. Bring to the boil and thicken, stirring well. Stir in the sugar, season to taste and pour the sauce over the ingredients in the casserole. Cook in a preheated moderate oven (350°F, 180°C, Gas Mark 4) for 1 hour. Meanwhile prepare the duchesse potatoes. Boil the potatoes, mash them well with butter. Lightly beat the egg yolk and mix it into the potato. Using a piping bag with large star nozzle, pipe a border of the mixture onto a serving dish. Garnish the potato border with sliced apricot halves and spoon the contents of the casserole into the centre. Sprinkle with flaked almonds and brown for 5 minutes under the grill, or 10 minutes in the oven.

12-oz. piece collar bacon
1 oz. butter
1 onion, sliced
1 green pepper
1 8-oz. can apricots
1 tablespoon cornflour
1 tablespoon vinegar
½ teaspoon soy sauce
2 oz. soft brown sugar
seasoning

Duchesse potatoes
8 oz. potatoes
½ oz. butter
1 egg yolk
1 oz. flaked almonds to garnish

Serves 4

Somerset pork (*above*)

Mrs. P. W. Swayne, Aley Farm, Over Stowey,
Bridgwater, Somerset

1 hand and spring of pork
3 oz. butter
1 onion, chopped
8 oz. celery, finely chopped
8 oz. long-grain rice
1 pint chicken stock
generous $\frac{1}{4}$ pint orange juice
3 oz. sultanas
grated rind of 1 orange
seasoning
2 oz. almonds, blanched and flaked
chopped parsley to garnish

Serves 6

Roast the pork in a preheated moderate oven (350°F,
180°C, Gas Mark 4) for 45 minutes per pound. About
10 minutes before meat is cooked melt 2 oz. of the
butter in a large frying pan and fry the onion and
celery until soft. Add the rice and fry until transparent. Add the chicken stock and orange juice and
simmer for 15 minutes. Meanwhile carve the pork
into small slices, without the crackling. Stir the pork
slices, the sultanas and orange rind into the rice and
cook together for 5 minutes. Adjust seasoning to
taste. Melt the remaining butter and fry the almonds
until golden brown. Add half of them to the rice mixture. Transfer the meat and rice to a serving dish,
arranging the best meat slices on the top. Garnish
with the rest of the almonds and the chopped parsley.

Note If the pork is cut into bite-sized pieces the
recipe makes a good hot buffet dish.
For a buffet meal or fork luncheon, the Somerset pork
can be served with a selection of salads – a green
salad and a tomato salad would be suitable.

Lamb and tomato casserole (*above*)

Mrs. Elizabeth Parker, 18 Welmore Road,
Glinton, Peterborough

Heat the oil in a frying pan and fry the sliced onion
until golden brown. Drain and place in the bottom of
a casserole. Divide the meat into about six pieces and
fry for 2–3 minutes, then transfer to the casserole.
Add the mixed vegetables. Pour the stock into the
frying pan, add the tomatoes, season and bring to the
boil. Pour over the casserole. Cover and cook in the
centre of a preheated moderate oven (325°F, 170°C,
Gas Mark 3) for 2 hours. Just before serving pour the
yogurt over the casserole.

2 tablespoons cooking oil
1 onion, sliced
1 lb. middle neck of lamb
8 oz. mixed vegetables, diced
(carrots, swede, celery, parsnips)
¼ pint meat stock
1 14-oz. can tomatoes
seasoning
1 5-oz. carton natural yogurt

Serves 3–4

Farmer's wife moussaka

Mrs. D. E. Newport, West Lodge, North Downs School, South Darenth, Nr. Dartford, Kent

Meat and tomato sauce
1 oz. butter
2 medium onions, chopped
1 clove garlic, crushed (optional)
1 lb. minced lamb or beef
1 15-oz. can tomatoes
3 tablespoons tomato purée
¼ teaspoon cinnamon
4 tablespoons red wine
1 tablespoon chopped parsley
¼ pint water

White sauce
1½ oz. butter
3 oz. flour
1 pint milk
salt and pepper
pinch nutmeg
1 egg and 2 yolks, beaten

2 aubergines
2 tablespoons cooking oil
2 oz. Cheddar cheese, grated
parsley to garnish

Serves 4–5

Prepare the meat and tomato sauce by melting the butter in a saucepan and frying the chopped onions until soft. Add the garlic (if used) and minced meat and fry for 5 minutes. Add the tomatoes, tomato purée, cinnamon, wine and parsley. Add the water and simmer for 1½ hours until the meat is cooked and the sauce is thick. Meanwhile make the white sauce; melt the butter and stir in the flour. Remove from the heat and gradually add the milk. Stir over the heat until the sauce thickens and boils. Remove the pan from the heat, cool slightly and season with salt, pepper and nutmeg. Beat in the eggs. Set the sauce aside with a layer of greaseproof paper pressed into the top to prevent a skin forming. Slice the aubergines and fry in oil until soft. Drain and set aside. To assemble the dish, use a deep casserole, and build up layers of aubergine, and meat sauce, ending with meat sauce. Pour the white sauce over the top, sprinkle with grated cheese and cook, uncovered in a preheated moderate oven (350°F, 180°C, Gas Mark 4) for 45 minutes – 1 hour until hot and bubbling. Garnish with parsley.

Croft fish casserole

Mrs. P. E. Shepherd, Croft Farm, Kenilworth

2 oz. butter
4 halibut or cod cutlets
4 oz. onion, chopped
1 oz. chives, chopped
1 oz. parsley, chopped
4 oz. mushrooms, chopped
juice of 1 lemon
¼ pint white wine
2 tablespoons tomato purée
2 egg yolks
¼ pint single cream or top of the milk

Serves 4

Spread the butter thickly over the base of a flame-proof dish. Add the fish cutlets, the onion, chives, parsley and mushrooms. Mix the lemon juice, white wine and tomato purée together and pour over the fish. Cover and cook gently for 15 minutes. Remove the cutlets and arrange on a serving dish, keeping them hot. Boil down the remaining liquid for 5–10 minutes. Remove from the heat and cool slightly. Beat the egg and cream, or top of the milk, together and stir into the liquid. Reheat the sauce, but do not boil and immediately pour over the fish. Garnish with lemon slices and parsley.

Note Any white fish can be used for this dish.

> *'The rule is jam tomorrow and jam yesterday, but never jam today.'*
>
> *Alice through the looking glass.*

Sweets.
A great variety of recipes were sent in for this section. It is encouraging to realize that the art of making desserts is not dying out, far from it—it's alive and well and flourishing in this book.

As with starters, it is important to make sure that the sweet complements the rest of the meal. For that reason, a selection of sweets has been included that gives you something suitable for every type of meal. Orange Fool would be a welcome follower to the more substantial dishes, whereas Westmorland Cheesecake or Peach Cheese Pie would go better after one of the lighter dishes, such as Farmhouse Chicken.

Surprisingly enough, the winning recipe for Caribbean Ice Cream comes all the way from sun-soaked Tregaron in Wales, but don't let that fool you. This sweet, with its hint of ginger will liven up any meal, and it's just as refreshing in winter as it is in summer. It would also make an ideal tea-time treat for children.

Other recipes in this section which deserve a special mention include: Mystery Pudding from Mrs. L. A. Keir in Kinellar, for its surprise element— crushed brandy snaps; Nottingham Pancake Layer from Mrs. A. Johnson of Bingham— you might like to try this one out next Shrove Tuesday; and finally, Suffolk Fruit Trifle, a classic English dessert which is always popular.

Some of these recipes involve cooking right up to the moment of serving. Others can be made in advance and left. So, when choosing a recipe, make sure there's enough time to do justice to the dish. Have you got plenty of eggs, cream, lemons and fresh fruit?

Then you're off. Good luck.

Mrs. P. Gregory, Pentrebwlen, Tregaron, Wales. Top
Mrs. N. Ebsworth, Morros Farm, Pendine, Wales. Bottom right
Mrs. A. Johnson, Starnhill Farm, Bingham, Notts. Bottom left
Mrs. G. Bennett, Lovehayne, Colyton, Devon. Middle right

Caribbean ice cream (*left*)

Mrs. P. Gregory, Pentrebwlen,
Llanddew-Brefi, Tregaron

Drain the pineapple pieces and put 4 tablespoons of the juice in a small pan. Add the sultanas, raisins and 3 tablespoons rum. Bring to the boil, cover and then simmer for 10 minutes. Leave to cool. Chop the pineapple pieces and ginger. Put the eggs and sugar in a bowl and place over a pan of hot water. Whisk over the hot water until the mixture is pale in colour and very thick. Whip the double cream until thickened, then gradually whisk in the single cream together with the syrup strained from the dried fruit, the remaining rum and the pineapple and ginger. Fold the cream mixture into egg mixture and pour into a freezing tray and freeze until half set; turn into a chilled bowl and whisk or stir thoroughly to distribute the fruit evenly. Freeze until firm then serve in small glasses (or a scooped-out pineapple) with ice cream wafer biscuits.

Variation Use apricots in place of the pineapple.

1 15-oz. can pineapple pieces
1 oz. sultanas
2 oz. raisins
4 tablespoons rum
2 pieces stem ginger
2 eggs
2 oz. castor sugar
$\frac{1}{4}$ pint double cream
$\frac{1}{4}$ pint single cream

Serves 4–6

Lemon and ginger bombe

Mrs. G. Bennett, Lovehayne, Southleigh,
Colyton, Devon

Beat the egg yolks with half the sugar until light and creamy. Beat in the milk and the remaining sugar; fold in the whipped cream and turn the mixture into an ice tray and freeze until the sides are firm. Turn out and beat again, adding the chopped ginger and stiffly beaten egg whites. Put a 1-pint pudding basin inside a $2\frac{1}{2}$-pint basin and fill the outer basin with the ginger ice cream mixture and freeze until firm. Boil the water, sugar and thinly pared lemon rind for the water ice for 10 minutes. Strain and when cool add the lemon juice and stiffly beaten egg white. Remove the smaller basin from the mixture and fill the cavity left with lemon mixture. Return to the freezer and freeze until firm. Turn out to serve.

Ginger ice cream
2 eggs, separated
8 oz. castor sugar
$\frac{1}{4}$ pint milk
$\frac{1}{2}$ pint double cream, whipped
2 oz. preserved ginger, chopped

Lemon water ice
$\frac{1}{2}$ pint water
3 oz. castor sugar
2 lemons
1 egg white

Serves 6

Marrons soufflé (*above*)

Mrs. T. Porter, Park Hill, Oswestry, Staffs

Put the chestnut purée, sherry, egg yolks, sugar and orange rind and juice in a bowl. Whisk (using an electric mixer, if available) until the mixture is thick and creamy. Dissolve the gelatine in 3 tablespoons of hot water. Whisking the mixture, gradually add the dissolved gelatine. Whip the cream until thickened and fold into the chestnut mixture. Finally fold in the stiffly beaten egg whites, using a metal tablespoon. Spoon the mixture into a prepared 6-inch soufflé dish and leave to set. Decorate with almonds and whipped cream.

1 can sweetened chestnut purée
2 tablespoons sherry
2 eggs, separated
2 oz. sugar
grated rind and juice of ½ orange
½ oz. gelatine
½ pint double cream
2 oz. almonds, chopped and whipped cream to decorate

Serves 4

Mystery pudding

Mrs. L. A. Keir, Aguhorsk, Kinellar, Aberdeenshire

Crush the brandy snaps into fairly small pieces. Whip the cream until thickened and fold in the brandy snap crumbs, the stiffly beaten egg whites and sugar. Chill for 3–4 hours before serving, decorated with walnut halves. If liked, extra chopped walnuts can be folded into the thickened cream.

4 oz. brandy snaps
½ pint double cream
4 egg whites
2 tablespoons castor sugar
walnut halves to decorate

Serves 4–5

44

Dreamy orange charlotte (*above*)

Mrs. M. Adams, Sunnycroft Farm, Pidley, Hants

4–5 oranges
1 lemon
8 oz. castor sugar
½ oz. powdered gelatine
2 tablespoons water
3 egg whites
½ pint double cream
2 tablespoons maraschino cherries
fresh fruit to decorate

Squeeze the juice from two of the oranges and the lemon and remove the pulp from one of the squeezed oranges. Place the juice and pulp in a pan, add the sugar, gelatine and water. Stir over a gentle heat until the gelatine has dissolved. Leave in the refrigerator or a cool place until the mixture starts to thicken. Peel the remaining oranges and divide into segments, removing all the skin and pith. Line a rinsed 8-inch ring mould with the orange segments. Whisk the chilled orange mixture until frothy and fold in the stiffly whisked egg whites. Whip the cream until thickened and fold into the orange mixture. Chop the cherries and add two-thirds of them to the mixture. Pour into the mould and leave to set. To serve, turn the mould out and fill the centre with fresh fruit and the remaining cherries. Serve with whipped cream.

Note If you do not have a ring mould the mixture can be placed in a serving dish and the fruit arranged on the top, or served separately.

Mocha desserts (*opposite*)

*Mrs. N. V. Ebsworth, Marros Farm,
Pendine, Carmarthen*

In a large bowl mix the cornflour, coffee and cocoa powder and sugar. Add the egg yolks and a little milk and blend until smooth. Heat the remaining milk with the butter to just below boiling point. Pour a little onto the mixture in the basin, mix well, then return to the milk in the pan. Stirring, bring to the boil and cook for 1–2 minutes. Spoon into six individual moulds or sundae glasses and leave to set in the refrigerator. To make the topping, whip the egg whites until stiff, add the cream, icing sugar and yogurt. Chill and spoon on top of the mocha desserts. Decorate with walnuts.

2½ oz. cornflour
2 teaspoons instant coffee powder
2 teaspoons cocoa powder
2 tablespoons castor sugar
2 eggs, separated
1½ pints milk
1 oz. butter

Topping
¼ pint single cream
2 tablespoons icing sugar
1 5-oz. carton natural yogurt
walnuts to decorate

Serves 6

Hazelnut gâteau

*Mrs. A. Wyles, Lamorna, Sibthorpe,
Newark, Notts*

Place 3 eggs and 3 oz. castor sugar in a bowl. Whisk together until the mixture becomes thick, light in colour and leaves a trail. Grind the hazelnuts in a liquidiser (or chop them finely) and fold 3 oz. into the whisked mixture. Spoon into a greased and lined 9-inch sandwich tin, smooth the top and bake in the centre of a preheated moderately hot oven (375°F, 190°C, Gas Mark 5) for 12–15 minutes. Turn out and cool on a wire tray. Make two more sponges in the same way, using 3 eggs etc. each time. To assemble the gâteau, whip the cream until thickened and sandwich the three cakes together with some of the cream and the jam. Smooth some cream on the top of the gâteau and pipe with the remaining cream. Decorate with hazelnuts.

9 eggs
9 oz. castor sugar
9 oz. hazelnuts
¾ pint double cream
about 4 oz. blackcurrant jam
hazelnuts to decorate

Serves 15

Note If you have a mixer 9 eggs and 9 oz. castor sugar can be whisked at one time. The sponges also freeze well and can be frozen when they have cooled completely. This makes a superb sweet for a buffet party. As an alternative filling to the blackcurrant jam, use fresh soft fruit when in season.

Orange fool

Mrs. B. Brinkler, The School House,
64 Uttoxeter Road, Rugeley, Staffs

Place the orange juice and eggs in a bowl and mix well together. Stir in the cream, nutmeg, cinnamon and sugar. Place the bowl over a pan of hot water and cook the mixture, stirring occasionally, until thickened. Pour into a serving dish and chill. Serve cold.

juice of 3 oranges
3 eggs, beaten
1 pint single cream
pinch nutmeg
pinch cinnamon
2½ oz. castor sugar

Serves 6

Marshmallow junket

Mrs. P. Lewis, Hobarris Farm,
Bucknell, Shrops

Heat (but do not boil) the milk and add the sugar. Stir in the marshmallows and when they begin to melt remove the pan from the heat. Whisk the mixture, then let it cool to blood heat and add the rennet. Leave the mixture to cool completely. If liked, serve with fruit and cream.

1 pint milk
1 tablespoon sugar
4 oz. marshmallows
2 teaspoons rennet

Serves 4

Note This is a very good sweet to serve after a rich main course dish.

Dairymaid's pudding

Mrs. D. Morris, Rymans Farm,
Brill, Aylesbury

Beat the egg yolks, egg white and sugar in a bowl.
Heat, but do not boil, the milk and pour onto the egg
mixture, stirring all the time. Place the bowl over a
pan of hot water and cook the mixture over a
moderate heat until it thickens, stirring frequently.
Put aside to cool, then freeze the custard until it is the
consistency of butter. Whip the cream until thickened and mix in the brandy or sherry to taste. Prepare
and chop the fruit and arrange in the bottom of a
mould. Add the cream and chopped nuts to the
custard and mix well together. Spoon into the mould,
pressing the mixture down well. Return to the
freezer. To serve, dip the mould in hot water for a
few seconds, then turn onto a serving dish.

6 egg yolks
1 egg white
4 oz. castor sugar
1 pint milk
½ pint double cream
brandy or sherry to taste
6 oz. fresh fruit, as available
½ oz. pistachio nuts, chopped
3 oz. almonds, chopped

Serves 10–12

Westmorland cheesecake

Mrs. K. Shepherd, 2 Gleblands Cottages,
Knock Appleby, Westmorland

Place the eggs and sugar in a bowl and put the bowl
over a pan of hot water. Whisk until the mixture is
thick and the whisk leaves a trail. Remove from the
heat and continue whisking until the mixture is cool.
Using a metal tablespoon, fold in the sieved flour.
Divide the mixture between two greased and floured
7-inch sandwich tins. Bake in the centre of a preheated moderately hot oven (375°F, 190°C, Gas
Mark 5) for 15 minutes. Turn out and cool on a wire
tray. To make the topping, sieve the cottage cheese
and beat with the cream, castor sugar and egg yolks.
Dissolve the gelatine in a little hot water and stir in
the lemon juice. Gradually add to the cheese mixture.
Whisk the egg whites until stiff and fold into the
mixture together with the sultanas. Return the cooled
cakes to the tins and divide the topping between
them. Leave in the refrigerator overnight.

2 eggs
3 oz. castor sugar
2 oz. self-raising flour, sieved

Topping
8 oz. cottage cheese
generous ¼ pint double cream
3 oz. castor sugar
2 eggs, separated
2 teaspoons gelatine
juice of 1 small lemon
2 oz. sultanas

Serves 8

Strawberry cheesecake (*above*)

Mrs. F. Crawford, Hillhead Dairy Dens,
Peterhead, Aberdeenshire

Melt the butter and stir in the crushed biscuits, brown sugar and cocoa powder. Press the crumb mixture in a 7-inch fluted flan ring placed on a baking tray, or a flan dish. Chill in the refrigerator. Whip the cream until thickened and add the yogurt. Combine the cream mixture with the cream cheese and castor sugar. Drain the strawberries and arrange three-quarters of them in the base of the flan. Smooth over the cream mixture and decorate with the remaining strawberries.

2 oz. butter
6 oz. digestive biscuits, crushed
1 oz. soft brown sugar
1 level teaspoon cocoa powder
¼ pint double cream
1 carton strawberry yogurt
3 oz. cream cheese
2 oz. castor sugar
1 8-oz. can strawberries, or fresh
strawberries
Serves 6

Peach cheese pie *(below)*

Mrs. S. M. Slater, Newhall,
Melrose, Roxburghshire

Crush the biscuits with a rolling pin (or blend in a liquidiser) and mix with the melted butter and 1 oz. of the sugar. Press the mixture into an 8-inch pie plate or flan dish. Drain the peaches and reserve the syrup. Beat together the cream cheese and remaining sugar until soft. Add the egg and egg yolk, lemon juice and vanilla essence; beat the mixture well and spoon into the prepared biscuit case. Bake in the centre of a preheated moderate oven (350°F, 180°C, Gas Mark 4) for 20–25 minutes, until filling is set. Leave to cool, then arrange the peach slices on the filling. Blend the arrowroot with the peach syrup and cook, stirring over a moderate heat, until thickened and clear. Cool slightly and spoon over the peaches. Leave to cool completely and serve decorated with whipped cream and crushed milk flake.

8 oz. digestive biscuits
4 oz. butter, melted
3 oz. castor sugar
1 8-oz. can sliced peaches
$4\frac{1}{2}$ oz. cream cheese
1 large egg plus 1 egg yolk
$\frac{1}{2}$ teaspoon lemon juice
1 teaspoon vanilla essence
2 teaspoons arrowroot
whipped cream and milk flake to decorate

Serves 6

Suffolk fruit trifle (*above*)

Mrs. J. R. Fidler, White House Farm,
Benhall, Saxmundham, Suffolk

Whisk the egg white until stiff and add the granulated
sugar. Whisk until stiff again, then fold in the castor
sugar. Using a star pipe, pipe the mixture onto a
lightly oiled baking tray. Place the meringues in a
preheated very cool oven (225°F, 110°C, Gas Mark $\frac{1}{4}$)
to dry out completely. Allow to cool. Break up the
sponge cakes and place in a large serving bowl. Drain
the peaches and pour the juice onto the trifle sponges.
Add the sherry, if used. Slice the bananas and peaches;
arrange on top of the sponges. Halve and pip the
grapes and halve the cherries; add to the bowl with
a little maraschino liquid. Pour over the cooled
custard and leave to become cold. Whip the cream
until thickened and spread over the custard; make a
pattern in the cream with blade of a knife and top
with the meringues. Decorate with cherries and
angelica.

1 egg white
1 oz. granulated sugar
1 oz. castor sugar
6 trifle sponge cakes
1 7-oz. can peaches
sherry to taste (optional)
3 bananas
4 oz. grapes
6 maraschino cherries
1 pint custard (pouring consistency)
$\frac{1}{4}$ pint double cream
cherries and angelica to decorate

Serves 8–10

Nottingham pancake layer (*above*)

Mrs. A. D. Johnson, Starnhill Farm,
Bingham, Notts

Sieve the flour into a bowl for the batter, stir in the sugar. Make a well in the middle of the dry ingredients and add the egg yolks. Beating with a wooden spoon, gradually mix in the egg yolks, milk, water and melted butter to form a smooth batter. Leave to stand for at least 2 hours. Just before using the batter, fold in the stiffly beaten egg whites. Peel, core and slice the apples and cook with the sugar over a gentle heat to form a thick apple sauce. Make 6-inch pancakes with the batter. To assemble the pancake layer, place one pancake on an ovenproof dish and spread with some of the apple sauce and sprinkle with a scant tablespoon of crushed macaroons. Add another pancake; continue in this way, ending with a pancake. Pour over the melted butter and sprinkle with the sugar. Cook in the centre of a preheated moderately hot oven (375°F, 190°C, Gas Mark 5) for 30 minutes, until heated through and the sugar just caramelised.

Batter
5 oz. plain flour
1 tablespoon castor sugar
3 eggs, separated
¼ pint milk
¼ pint water
2½ oz. butter, melted
fat for frying

Filling
2 lb. cooking apples
3 oz. granulated sugar
3 oz. macaroons, crushed

Topping
1 oz. butter, melted
2 tablespoons granulated sugar

Serves 6

Gooseberry king of puddings (*above*)

Mrs. Millar, 161 Castlecat Road,
Ballymoney, Co. Antrim

Top and tail the gooseberries and cook in a pan with a
little water and half the granulated sugar until soft.
Leave to cool. Place the milk and butter in a pan and
bring to the boil. Remove from the heat, cool slightly
and stirring, pour onto the egg yolks and remaining
sugar in a bowl. Mix the cooled gooseberries with the
breadcrumbs and place in a greased pie dish. Strain
over the custard. Place the pie dish in a roasting tin
half filled with water and bake in the centre of a preheated moderate oven (350°F, 180°C, Gas Mark 4)
for 30 minutes. Remove and leave to cool. Increase
the oven heat to hot (425°F, 220°C, Gas Mark 7).
Heat the gooseberry jam and smooth it over the
baked custard. Whip the egg whites until stiff and
fold in the castor sugar. Pipe or smooth the meringue
over the jam, covering it completely. Return to the
hot oven to brown the meringue. Serve, hot or cold,
with whipped cream.

8 oz. fresh gooseberries
4 oz. granulated sugar
1 pint milk
2 oz. butter
2 eggs
4 oz. fresh white breadcrumbs
1 oz. gooseberry jam
2 oz. castor sugar

Serves 4

> *'If ever I ate a good supper at night,*
> *I dreamed of the devil and wakened in fright.'*
>
> Christopher Anstey, the New Bath Guide.

Suppers.

You'll find that none of the supper dishes included here will give you nightmares. What they will give you is a selection of meals and snacks that are cheaper and quicker to prepare than most of the main courses in this book. But these are not substitute dishes, they are every bit as nourishing and just as wholesome as the main courses.

With most of them, you can do the preparation and cooking hours in advance, and leave them, hot or cold, to be snapped up by hungry children and husbands any time they feel like a bite.

Mrs. N. Jones of Llandysul is the second winner in this book to come from Wales. Her Welsh Lamb Casserole is a very original dish, and it would be ideal to serve with a potato baked in its jacket, split open and topped with fresh butter, salt, black pepper and chives.

If you are looking for economical meals that are nourishing as well, we suggest you try the Irish Cauliflower, the Cheese and Onion Pasties, or the Antrim Egg Supper. If any of your children are learning to cook, you could start them off on these dishes; they're not difficult to make, and the results are very rewarding.

The fact that all these dishes come under the heading of suppers, doesn't mean that they have to be eaten between 7 and 10 pm. Bacon and egg pie would be just as welcome at breakfast, on a picnic, or as a midday meal.

Be brave and experiment with your cooking, but remember one simple rule: your meals can only be as good as the food that goes into them. So always use the freshest and best country produce that it is possible to find.

Mrs. P. Bugg, Kingsford Farm, Exeter, Devon. Middle right
Mrs. J. Sharley, Lower Burlestone Farm, Dartmouth, S. Devon. Top
Mrs. S. Thorogood, Penhill Farm, Cheltenham, Gloucester. Middle left
Mrs. M. Wilson, Mains of Dellavaird, Kincardineshire, Scotland. Bottom

Welsh lamb casserole (*left*)

Mrs. N. Jones, Llwyn-Eos,
Rhydlewis, Llandysul

1 oz. butter
2 cloves garlic, crushed
2 onions, sliced
2 aubergines, sliced
1 14-oz. can tomatoes
12 oz. cooked lamb, minced
½ teaspoon oregano
½ teaspoon rosemary
salt and black pepper
2 5-oz. cartons natural yogurt
3 egg yolks
1 oz. cheese, grated
parsley to garnish

Serves 4

Melt the butter in a flameproof casserole. Add the garlic, onions and aubergines and cook gently for 10–15 minutes, stirring occasionally. Add the tomatoes, lamb, oregano and rosemary. Add salt and pepper to taste and stir well. Cover and cook gently for 10 minutes. Put the yogurt in a small pan and beat until smooth. Beat in the egg yolks and heat very gently until the mixture thickens – do not allow it to boil. Pour the yogurt mixture over the contents of the casserole, sprinkle with grated cheese and cook, uncovered, in the centre of a preheated moderate oven (350°F, 180°C, Gas Mark 4) for 30 minutes. Garnish with parsley.

Game soufflé

Mrs. S. K. Thorogood, Penhill Farm,
Colesbourne, Cheltenham

3 oz. butter
8 oz. onions, thinly sliced
6–8 oz. cooked pheasant
½ teaspoon thyme
1 teaspoon chopped parsley
1 oz. flour
½ pint milk
salt and pepper
3 tablespoons single cream
3 eggs, separated

Serves 4

Melt 1 oz. of the butter and fry the onions until soft. Stir in the diced pheasant, thyme and parsley. Place in the bottom of a greased 2½-pint soufflé dish. Melt the remaining butter in a pan, remove from the heat and stir in the flour. Gradually stir in the milk, return the pan to the heat and, stirring, bring to the boil and cook for 2 minutes. Add seasoning to taste. Add half the sauce and the cream to the pheasant and onion mixture. Beat the egg yolks into the remaining sauce. Whisk the egg whites until stiff and fold them into the sauce mixture. Place on top of the mixture in the soufflé dish and bake in the centre of a preheated moderately hot oven (375°F, 190°C, Gas Mark 5) for about 40 minutes, until well risen. Serve at once.

Note This is a very good way of using up cold roast game or poultry.

Haymakers' snack (left)

Mrs. R. Evans, Tyisa-Dinam,
Llandrillo, Merioneth

1 oz. butter
2 rashers bacon, finely chopped
1 small leek, chopped
8 oz. mashed potato
salt and pepper
2 tablespoons chopped parsley
2 eggs
8 oz. skinless sausages, cooked
4 oz. fresh white breadcrumbs
fat or oil for deep frying
watercress to garnish

Serves 4

Melt the butter in a pan and gently fry the chopped bacon and leek until cooked. Place the potato (which should be fairly dry) in a bowl and add the bacon, leek, seasoning and chopped parsley. Beat in one of the eggs. With floured hands, form a portion of the potato mixture around each sausage. Lightly beat the remaining egg and coat each potato-sausage in egg and breadcrumbs, pressing them on well. Fry in heated fat or oil, until golden brown on all sides. Drain on absorbent paper and serve hot, garnished with watercress.

Note A pinch of mixed herbs can be added with the parsley.

Sausage salad snack

Mrs. D. M. Proctor, 10 Vicarage Lane, Tillingham,
Southminster, Essex

1 5-oz. carton natural yogurt
1 lb. dessert apples
$\frac{1}{2}$ cucumber
3 oz. gherkins, chopped
3 oz. stoned raisins, chopped
8–10 cold cooked sausages
parsley to garnish

Serves 4–5

Place the yogurt in a bowl, chop the apples and unpeeled cucumber into $\frac{1}{2}$-inch pieces and stir into the yogurt. Mix in the gherkins and raisins. Chill in the refrigerator for 1 hour. Slice the sausages and arrange around the edge of a serving dish. Pile the yogurt mixture in the centre, garnish with parsley and serve with bread or rolls crisped in the oven.

Note Frankfurters can be used in place of sausages.

Yogurt surprise

Mrs. E. Hall, Tween Farm,
Fenwick, Doncaster

4 thick slices white bread
2 oz. butter
2 tablespoons chutney
1 5-oz. carton natural yogurt
1 egg, beaten
3 oz. cheese, grated
salt and pepper
tomato slices and parsley

Serves 4

Toast the bread slices on both sides and spread one side of each slice with butter. Spread thickly with chutney. Mix the yogurt, egg and cheese in a bowl and season to taste. Divide the yogurt mixture between the slices of toast. Just before serving, put under a moderate grill to heat through and brown the top. Garnish with tomato slices and chopped parsley.

Note If liked, the chutney can be replaced by a slice of ham spread with French mustard.

Devilled ham rolls (*below*)

Mrs. M. Wilson, Mains of Dellavaird,
Laurencekirk, Kincardineshire

Drain the sweetcorn, mix with the French dressing
and leave on one side. Cut the potatoes, one of the
apples, unpeeled, and the cucumber into $\frac{1}{4}$-inch
pieces. Beat the cream cheese until softened, then
beat in the mustard and milk. Stir in the prepared
potatoes, apple and cucumber. Season to taste and
divide the mixture between the slices of ham and roll
them up. Arrange the sweetcorn on a large serving
dish and place the filled ham rolls on top. Garnish
with the remaining apple, sliced and dipped in lemon
juice, and with sprigs of watercress.

1 11-oz. can sweetcorn
4 tablespoons French dressing
2 large potatoes, cooked until just
tender
2 red-skinned dessert apples
2-inch piece cucumber
6 oz. cream cheese
2 teaspoons made mustard
3 tablespoons milk
salt and pepper
8 thin slices cooked ham
little lemon juice
watercress to garnish

Serves 4

Savoury bacon crumble

Mrs. T. M. Anderson Mobbs, Crossways Farm,
Corton, Lowestoft

8 oz. bacon rashers
1 large onion, sliced
1 lb. potatoes, peeled and sliced
4 oz. mushrooms, sliced
8 oz. tomatoes, sliced
salt and pepper
¼ pint water
1 oz. butter

Crumble
2 oz. butter
4 oz. plain flour
salt and pepper
tomato slices and parsley to garnish

Serves 3–4

Remove the rinds from the bacon rashers and cut the rashers in half. Arrange layers of sliced onion, potato, mushrooms and tomato in a deep 8–9-inch casserole dish, seasoning each layer. Add the water, and the butter cut in small pieces. Cover and cook in the centre of a preheated moderate oven (350°F, 180°C, Gas Mark 4) for about 1 hour, until the potatoes are softened. Make the crumble by rubbing the butter into the flour and seasoning. Remove the casserole from the oven, cool slightly, then spread the crumble mixture over the top. Increase the oven temperature to moderately hot (400°F, 200°C, Gas Mark 6) and return the dish, uncovered, to the oven and cook for a further 30 minutes. Serve garnished with tomato slices and parsley.

Bacon and egg pie

Mrs. H. Rendall, Lee Farm,
Patching, Worthing

8 oz. shortcrust pastry
½ oz. butter
4 oz. bacon
1 large onion, sliced
1 tomato, sliced
salt and pepper
squeeze of lemon juice
4–5 eggs
2 oz. Cheddar cheese, grated
milk to glaze

Serves 4–6

Use about two-thirds of the pastry to line an 8-inch greased pie dish and bake blind in the centre of a preheated moderate oven (350°F, 180°C, Gas Mark 4) for 10–15 minutes. Meanwhile melt the butter in a pan and fry the bacon, cut into small strips; remove and fry the onion. Arrange the bacon in the bottom of the pastry case and cover with the onion. Add the tomato slices, salt and pepper and lemon juice. Break the eggs on top and sprinkle with grated cheese. Roll out the remaining pastry and use to cover the pie. Flute the edges and make a centre decoration with the pastry trimmings. Brush with milk and bake in the centre of the moderate oven for about 40 minutes.

Market day flan

Mrs. P. A. O. Bugg, Kingsford Farm,
Longdown, Exeter

6 oz. shortcrust pastry
4–6 rashers streaky bacon
1 onion, chopped
1 egg plus 1 egg yolk
1 5-oz. carton natural yogurt
4 oz. cheese, grated
pinch dried herbs
salt and pepper

Serves 6

Line an 8-inch flan ring with the pastry. Fry the chopped bacon in its own fat. Add the chopped onion and cook slowly until onion is soft and transparent. Cool and place over the base of the flan. Beat the eggs together and add the yogurt, cheese, herbs and salt and pepper. Pour into the flan and bake in the centre of a preheated moderately hot oven (375°F, 190°C, Gas Mark 5) for 30 minutes. Garnish with tomato slices and parsley.

Cheese and onion pasties

Mrs. M. Eddols, New Duston, Northampton

10 oz. plain flour
2½ oz. lard
2½ oz. butter
5 oz. cheese, grated
cold water to mix

Filling
1 onion, finely chopped
4 oz. cheese, grated
4 oz. potatoes, mashed
2–3 tomatoes, diced
salt and pepper
beaten egg to glaze

Makes 8

Sieve the flour into a bowl. Rub in the lard and butter until the mixture resembles fine breadcrumbs. Stir in the grated cheese and mix to a stiff dough with cold water. Mix together the filling ingredients and season well. Divide the pastry into eight portions and roll each piece out to a circle a ¼ inch thick. Cut each into a 6-inch round. Divide the filling between the circles, moisten the edges and bring them together; flute and place on a baking tray, prick the pasties and brush with beaten egg. Bake on the second shelf of a preheated moderately hot oven (400°F, 200°C, Gas Mark 6) for 25–30 minutes. Serve hot or cold.

Yorkshire potato scones *(left)*

Mrs. A. M. Forbes, High Caythorpe Farm, Driffield

4 oz. self-raising flour
pinch salt
1 teaspoon baking powder
1 oz. butter
4 oz. cold mashed potato
2 oz. mushrooms, chopped
milk to mix and glaze

Makes 10

Sieve the flour, salt and baking powder into a bowl. Rub in the butter. Stir in the potato, cooked mushrooms and sufficient milk to mix to a soft dough consistency. Roll out the mixture to a ½-inch thickness and cut into triangles. Place on a greased baking tray, brush with milk and bake on the second shelf from the top of a preheated hot oven (425°F, 220°C, Gas Mark 7) for 15–20 minutes. Serve hot.

Antrim egg supper (*left*)

Mrs. E. M. Shannon, Newtonabbey, Co. Antrim

Melt the butter for the cheese sauce in a pan and stir in the flour. Cook for 1–2 minutes, stirring. Remove from the heat and gradually stir in the milk. Return to the heat and stirring all the time, bring to the boil to thicken. Stir in the cheese, and heat gently to melt the cheese. Break the cauliflower into florets and arrange in the base of a shallow ovenproof dish. Season and pour on the cheese sauce. Make four hollows with the back of a spoon and carefully break an egg into each. Sprinkle with grated cheese and bake in the centre of a preheated moderately hot oven (375°F, 190°C, Gas Mark 5) for 15 minutes, until the eggs are set.

1 cauliflower, cooked
salt and pepper
4 eggs
1 oz. cheese, grated

Cheese sauce
1½ oz. butter
1½ oz. flour
1 pint milk
4 oz. cheese, grated

Serves 4

Irish cauliflower

Mrs. Gash, Sunview Farm, Ballyfeard, Co. Cork

Make a white sauce with the butter, flour and milk. Add the seasoning and three-quarters of the cheese; allow the cheese to melt, then remove from the heat and allow to cool. Beat in the egg yolks, then fold in the stiffly beaten egg whites. Make layers starting with cauliflower florets, tomato slices and the cheese mixture in an ovenproof dish, ending with a layer of cheese mixture. Sprinkle with the remaining cheese. Cook in the centre of a preheated moderately hot oven (400°F, 200°C, Gas Mark 6) for 30 minutes until well risen and set. Serve at once.

1 oz. butter
1 oz. flour
½ pint milk
salt and pepper
1½ oz. cheese, grated
1 cauliflower, cooked
2 eggs, separated
3 tomatoes, sliced

Serves 4

Red sunset

Mrs. J. Sharley, Lower Burlestone Farm, Dartmouth

Trim the cabbage, cut into quarters and remove the centre stalk. Slice into ¼-inch strips. Melt the dripping in a pan and add the cabbage, apple and onion. Cover and simmer over a low heat for 30–40 minutes, until the cabbage is just tender – not soggy. Place the mixture on a serving dish and serve hot, with the yogurt spooned over the top.

1 red cabbage
1 oz. dripping
1 large apple, sliced
1 large onion, sliced
salt and pepper
1 5-oz. carton natural yogurt

Serves 4

Note This dish is also delicious served cold.

Fish fillets with cider sauce (*below*)

Mrs. D. E. Reed, Milford, Honiton, Devon

1½ lb. sole or plaice fillets
generous ¼ pint dry cider
3 tablespoons water
1 oz. butter
1 tablespoon flour
salt and pepper
squeeze of lemon juice
1 tablespoon chopped parsley
1–2 tablespoons single cream
lemon slices and parsley to garnish

Serves 4

Fold the fillets, skin sides inside, and place them in a lightly greased ovenproof dish. Pour over the cider and water, cover with foil or a butter paper and cook in the centre of a preheated moderate oven (350°F, 180°C, Gas Mark 4) for 12–15 minutes. Melt the butter in a pan. Remove from the heat and stir in the flour; cook, stirring, over a moderate heat for 1 minute. Strain in the fish liquor. Stirring all the time, bring to the boil and simmer for 3–4 minutes. Season to taste and add the lemon juice, parsley and cream. Arrange the fish on a serving dish and coat with sauce. Garnish with lemon slices and parsley and serve at once.

Sardine tart

Mrs. J. M. Harry, The Villa, South Somercotes, Louth, Lincs

6 oz. shortcrust pastry
1 can sardines in oil
1 small onion, finely sliced
juice of ½ lemon
1 5-oz. carton natural yogurt
2 eggs
freshly ground black pepper
parsley to garnish

Serves 4

Roll out the pastry and use to line an 8-inch fluted flan ring. Drain the oil from the sardines into a small pan and fry the onion rings in it until soft. Drain and arrange the onion rings on the base of the flan and sprinkle with half the lemon juice. Beat together the yogurt and eggs and pour into the flan case. Arrange the sardines on top, like the spokes of a wheel. Sprinkle with the remaining lemon juice and some freshly ground black pepper. Bake in the centre of a preheated hot oven (425°F, 220°C, Gas Mark 7) for 15 minutes, then reduce heat to moderate (350°F, 180°C, Gas Mark 4) and then cook for a further 25 minutes. Serve hot or cold, garnished with parsley.

Hot cross fish cakes

Mrs. B. Hansard, Cater Lane Farm, Thornton-le-Moor, Lincoln

Fish cakes
12 oz. cooked white fish
8 oz. mashed potato
2 oz. cheese, grated
salt and pepper
milk to mix (optional)

Coating
1 egg
4 oz. breadcrumbs
fat or oil for deep frying

Crosses
1 egg
1 tablespoon milk
watercress to garnish

Serves 5

Remove the skin and bones from the fish and flake the fish in a bowl. Add the mashed potato, cheese and seasoning to taste. Use a little milk if necessary, to form a fairly soft consistency. Form the mixture into 10 cakes and coat each one in beaten egg and then in breadcrumbs; press the coating on well. Fry the cakes, a few at a time, in heated fat or oil for 5–10 minutes, until golden brown. Drain on absorbent paper and keep hot. Scramble the egg with the milk until just thickened and remove from the heat. Use the egg mixture to make a cross on each fish cake and serve at once, garnished with watercress.

Note Any cooked white fish is suitable for this recipe; try haddock, cod or hake. Alternatively, canned, drained salmon can be used, in which case add a few drops of lemon juice to the mixture.

'Scotland – land o' cakes.'

Robert Burns.

Cakes.
200 years later, Scotland is still the land of cakes.

The winner in this section comes from Kirkcaldy, in Fife, and another finalist comes from Coldstream, in Berwick. But apart from that, the recipes come from far afield; two from Ireland, three from Wales, one from Devon, one from Essex, and several from the North of England. So the saying really ought to be, the British Isles, land of cakes.

Baking a cake is the test of any cook's skill. But as well as that, it should be an enjoyable and rewarding experience. The most important ingredient in any of the recipes is time, you just can't afford to take short cuts. Then you'll need a good supply of fresh country produce; new laid eggs and creamy butter can do a lot to raise a cake from the mediocre to the superb.

It's always advisable to put the oven on before beginning. This ensures that the cake is cooked at an even temperature from start to finish. And when the cake does go in, there's a long pleasant wait while the aroma drifts through the house, making mouths water. The smell of a rich fruit cake cooking in a farmhouse kitchen on a cold winter morning takes a lot of beating.

The winning recipe, Clunie Cake, was submitted by Mrs. J. Clark of Clunie Mains, Kirkcaldy. It's an exciting mixture of biscuits, cream and pineapple. It's easy to make, and quite quick, although it will need some time to cool down. There's an old saying that the test of a good cake is how long it lasts, the shorter the time, the better the cake. We think that Clunie Cake will be so popular that it won't last more than a few hours.

Biscuits go down well at any time of the day, but there's no need to buy them when you can make some Ruddy's Breaks so easily. They won't last long either, so you could make some Maltkiln Bread too. This loaf really is superb, it's based on a traditional recipe and is a cross between malt loaf and a plum pudding. It's extremely tasty.

There is one final word of warning— good cakes are addictive, and just occasionally they can be a little bit fattening. So whatever the temptations, watch your weight!

Mrs. J. Clark, Clunie Mains, Kirkcaldy, Scotland. Bottom
Mrs. G. Brydon, Sunilaws Farm, Coldstream, Berwickshire. Middle right
Mrs. S. J. Black, Leigh Barton, Exeter, Devon. Top
Mrs. J. Harrison, Ramper Farm, Skegness, Lincs. Middle left

Clunie cake (above)

*Mrs. J. Clark, Clunie Mains,
Kirkcaldy, Fife*

Cream the butter and sugar together until light and fluffy. Mix in the biscuit crumbs, breadcrumbs, flour and ground almonds and knead the mixture lightly. Divide it in two and press each piece into an 8-inch fluted flan ring placed on a baking tray. Bake each round in the centre of a preheated moderate oven (325°F, 170°C, Gas Mark 3) for 20 minutes. Cool on a wire tray. Whip the cream lightly and into half of it fold the drained pineapple pieces. Sandwich the two rounds together with this mixture. Sprinkle the top with icing sugar and decorate with the remaining whipped cream and the pineapple rings.

7 oz. butter
2 oz. castor sugar
4 oz. biscuit crumbs
4 oz. toasted breadcrumbs
5 oz. plain flour
2½ oz. ground almonds
½ pint double cream
1 small can pineapple pieces, drained
pineapple rings to decorate

Pineapple brown sponge cake

Mrs. J. Bell, Moorside, Thornton-le-Moor,
Northallerton

3 eggs
3 oz. dark brown sugar
3 oz. plain flour, sieved

Filling
1 small can pineapple rings
½ pint double cream
½ teaspoon vanilla essence
1 tablespoon dark brown sugar

Decoration
chopped nuts
glacé cherries

Whisk the eggs and sugar together in a warm bowl until thick and creamy – this takes about 15–20 minutes. Lightly fold in the flour and divide the mixture between two greased and base-lined 7-inch sandwich tins. Bake in the centre of a preheated moderate oven (350°F, 180°C, Gas Mark 4) for 30–40 minutes. Turn out and cool on a wire tray. Drain the pineapple rings well and chop them, reserving one whole ring for decoration. Whip the cream and to half of it add the chopped pineapple, vanilla essence and dark brown sugar. Use this to sandwich the two cakes together. Spread some of the remaining cream around the sides of the cake and roll the sides in the chopped nuts. Smooth the remaining cream on the top of the cake and decorate with the reserved pineapple and glacé cherries.

Note These cakes can be stored in an airtight tin, before being filled and decorated.

Kirsch delight

Mrs. Y. Prescott, Wold House Lund,
Driffield, E. Yorks

Genoese pastry
3 large eggs
3 oz. castor sugar
3 oz. plain flour
1 oz. butter, melted

Filling
4 oz. butter
4 oz. icing sugar, sieved
1 tablespoon double cream
2 teaspoons Kirsch

Decoration
chocolate vermicelli
2 oz. plain chocolate

Grease and line two 6½-inch sandwich tins. Place the eggs and sugar in a bowl and whisk them together until thick and creamy. Fold in the sieved flour and the melted butter. Divide the mixture between the prepared tins, smooth the tops and bake in the centre of a preheated moderate oven (325°F, 170°C, Gas Mark 3) for about 35 minutes. Turn out and cool on a wire tray. Cream the butter and icing sugar together for the filling. Beat in the cream and Kirsch. Sandwich the cooled cakes together with half the filling. Spread half the remainder around the sides and roll the sides in vermicelli. Melt the chocolate in a basin placed over a pan of hot water and smooth it over the top of the cake. When set, pipe the top edge of the cake with rosettes of the remaining filling.

Chocolate crumbow (*right*)

Mrs. M. Brown, Titlington Mount, Northumberland

Crush the biscuits finely with a rolling pin. Cream the butter and sugar together until light and fluffy. Separate the eggs and beat the yolks into the creamed mixture. Melt the chocolate in a bowl placed over a pan of hot water; stir into the creamed mixture and mix well, then fold in the stiffly beaten egg whites. Put a layer of crumbs in the base of a 1-lb. loaf tin, then a layer of the chocolate mixture; continue building up the layers, ending with a layer of crumbs. When set turn out and if liked, pipe with whipped cream.

9 oz. coconut macaroon biscuits
6 oz. butter
3 tablespoons castor sugar
4 eggs
7 oz. cooking chocolate
¼ pint double cream to decorate (optional)

Serves 8–10

Irish coffee cake

Mrs. E. M. Shannon, Mallusk, Co. Antrim

Cream the butter and sugar together until light and fluffy. Gradually beat in the egg yolks and milk. Sieve the flour, cornflour and baking powder together and fold into the creamed mixture. Fold in the stiffly beaten egg whites. Spoon the mixture into a greased and bottom-lined 8-inch cake tin. Bake in the centre of a preheated moderately hot oven (375°F, 190°C, Gas Mark 5) for 20 minutes. Lower the heat to moderate (325°F, 170°C, Gas Mark 3) and bake for a further 25–30 minutes. Turn out and cool on a wire tray. When cool return the cake to the tin in which it was cooked and prick it all over with a fine skewer. To make the coffee syrup, put the coffee and sugar in a small saucepan. Stir until the sugar has dissolved, then boil quickly for 5 minutes. Remove the pan from the heat and stir in the whiskey. Pour the hot syrup over the cake and leave it to soak in. When cold, cover and leave overnight. Decorate with cream and almonds.

4½ oz. butter or margarine
7 oz. castor sugar
2 eggs, separated
6 tablespoons milk
4½ oz. plain flour
2 oz. cornflour
3 teaspoons baking powder

Coffee syrup
¼ pint strong black coffee or 4 teaspoons instant coffee powder dissolved in ¼ pint hot water
4 oz. demerara sugar
2–3 tablespoons Irish whiskey

Decoration
½ pint double cream
4 oz. almonds, toasted

Serves 8–10

72

Celebration cake (*above*)

Mrs. J. Sterland, Moor Farm,
Coleorton, Leicester

8 oz. rich tea biscuits
8 oz. plain chocolate
8 oz. butter
2 egg yolks
2 tablespoons rum
1 teaspoon vanilla essence
1 tablespoon instant coffee
powder or granules
3 tablespoons single cream
8 oz. icing sugar
2 oz. flaked almonds

Decoration
¼ pint double cream
few almonds, browned

Break the biscuits into small pieces. Melt the chocolate in a bowl placed over a pan of hot water. Add the butter, a little at a time. Remove the bowl from the heat and add the egg yolks, rum and vanilla essence. Stir the coffee powder or granules into the cream, then stir into the chocolate mixture. Fold in the biscuit pieces, icing sugar and almonds. Smooth the mixture into a greased and lined 7-inch cake tin. Press down well and leave in the refrigerator overnight. The next day, turn out of the tin and decorate with whipped cream and browned almonds.

Cherry cheesecake (*below*)

Mrs. G. Brydon, Sunilaws Farm,
Coldstream, Berwickshire

Mix together the biscuit crumbs, granulated sugar and melted butter. Press the mixture into the base of a loose-bottomed 8-inch cake tin. Bake in the centre of a preheated moderate oven (350°F, 180°C, Gas Mark 4) for 10 minutes. Leave to cool. Beat the cream cheese and icing sugar together until creamy. Whip the cream until thickened and fold into the cheese mixture. Spread evenly over the cooked crumb base. When set spread the pie filling over the top and leave to chill, prefer- ably overnight. Turn onto a dish to serve.

5 oz. digestive biscuit crumbs
2 tablespoons granulated sugar
4 oz. butter, melted
4 oz. cream cheese
4 oz. icing sugar
½ pint double cream
1 can cherry pie filling

Serves 6–8

Lemon ice box cake

Mrs. N. E. Cullington, Tickton House,
Nr. Beverley, E. Yorks

Place the eggs and sugar in a bowl and put the bowl over a pan of hot water. Whisk the eggs and sugar together until thick and mousse-like. (If using an electric mixer, there is no need to whisk the mixture over hot water.) Remove the bowl from the saucepan and continue whisking until the mixture is cool. Fold in the sieved flour and turn the mixture into a greased and lined 8-inch cake tin. Smooth the top and bake in the centre of a preheated moderately hot oven (375°F, 190°C, Gas Mark 5) for 25 minutes. Turn out and cool on a wire tray. Beat the egg yolks with 6 oz. of the sugar and add the lemon rind and juice and boil- ing water. Cook the mixture in a double saucepan (or a bowl placed over a pan of hot water) until thick-

3 eggs
4 oz. castor sugar
3 oz. plain flour, sieved

Filling
4 eggs, separated
10 oz. castor sugar
grated rind and juice of
2 lemons
3 tablespoons boiling water
½ oz. gelatine
3 tablespoons warm water
½ pint double cream and
crystallised lemon slices
to decorate

ened. Soak the gelatine in the warm water and add to the lemon mixture. Beat the egg whites with the remaining sugar until thick, then fold into the lemon mixture. Cut cooled cake into three layers. Line an 8-inch cake tin with greaseproof paper and place one layer of sponge in the bottom. Add a layer of lemon mixture, then another sponge layer. Continue with these layers, ending with a layer of sponge. Leave to set in the refrigerator. To serve, turn out and cover the top and sides with whipped cream. Decorate with crystallised lemon slices.

Nutty chocolate gâteau (above)

Mrs. J. Shanks, 'The Highlands', Ballymacarn, Co. Down

Gâteau
4 large eggs
9 oz. castor sugar
6 oz. plain flour
2 tablespoons cocoa powder
2 teaspoons baking powder
5 tablespoons milk
2 oz. butter

Filling
1 lb. icing sugar
1 oz. drinking chocolate powder
4 oz. butter
4 tablespoons milk
3 oz. almonds or walnuts, chopped
chocolate vermicelli to decorate

Serves 10–12

Beat the eggs lightly. Gradually add the sugar and beat the mixture until thick and creamy. Sieve the flour, cocoa powder and baking powder twice. Using a metal tablespoon, lightly fold the sieved flour mixture into the egg mixture. Heat the milk and butter together to melt the butter, then fold into the mixture. Divide the mixture between two greased and floured 8-inch sandwich tins. Bake in the centre of a preheated moderately hot oven (375°F, 190°C, Gas Mark 5) for 30–35 minutes. Turn out and cool on a wire tray. When cold split each cake in half through the centre. Sieve the icing sugar and drinking chocolate powder together. Melt the butter, remove from the heat and add the milk. Gradually add the butter and milk mixture to the sieved icing sugar and drinking chocolate powder and beat together to form a soft smooth mixture. Cover the bottom layer of cake with one quarter of the filling and sprinkle over 1 oz. of the nuts. Place another round of cake on top. Continue to build the gâteau up in layers. Decorate the sides and top with the remaining icing and sprinkle with chocolate vermicelli.

Devon apple loaf (*below*)

Mrs. J. Black, Leigh Barton,
Silverton, Exeter

Peel, core and chop the apples. Cook them in a little water to give ½ pint apple purée. Sieve the flour (or flour and baking powder) into a bowl. Rub in the butter until the mixture resembles fine breadcrumbs. Add the sugar, cinnamon, dates and nuts. Then add the apple purée and lastly the milk. Mix well and spoon into a greased 2-lb. loaf tin. Bake in the centre of a preheated cool oven (300°F, 150°C, Gas Mark 2) for about 1¼ hours. Turn out and cool on a wire tray. If liked, decorate the top with apple slices and glacé icing.

1 lb. cooking apples
12 oz. self-raising flour
(preferably wholewheat)
or 12 oz. plain flour and
1½ teaspoons baking powder
6 oz. butter
6 oz. soft brown sugar
1 teaspoon ground cinnamon
8 oz. dates, chopped
4 oz. hazelnuts, chopped
2–3 tablespoons milk
* apple slices dipped in lemon*
*   juice and glacé icing to*
*   decorate (optional)*

Wholemeal fruit loaf

Mrs. C. Blackwaters, High Barn Hall,
Halstead, Essex

Put all the ingredients, except the flour and baking powder, into a bowl. Mix thoroughly and leave for 1 hour. Stir in the flour and baking powder and spoon the mixture into a lined and greased 2-lb. loaf tin. Smooth the top and bake in the centre of a preheated moderate oven (325°F, 170°C, Gas Mark 3) for 1¼–1½ hours. Cool in the tin slightly, then turn out and finish cooling on a wire tray. The following day, cut into slices and spread with butter.

3 oz. All-bran
3 oz. soft brown sugar
6 oz. mixed dried fruit
½ pint milk
1 large cooking apple, grated
6 oz. wholemeal flour
1 teaspoon baking powder

Maltkiln bread

Mrs. J. A. Lane, Maltkiln Farm,
Normandy-by-Spital, Lincoln

¾ oz. dried yeast
¼ pint lukewarm water
1½ teaspoons sugar
1¾ lb. strong plain flour
¾ teaspoon salt
6 oz. lard
10 oz. currants
4 oz. raisins
2 oz. sultanas
1 oz. chopped peel
6 oz. sugar
2 eggs, beaten
about ¾ pint lukewarm milk

Glaze
2 tablespoons sugar
2 tablespoons milk

Put the dried yeast, lukewarm water and sugar in a small bowl. Leave to stand in a warm place for 15 minutes. Sieve the flour and salt into a warmed bowl. Rub in the lard, then add the currants, raisins, sultanas, peel and sugar. Mix the dry ingredients together and make a well in the centre. Pour in the beaten eggs, milk and yeast liquid and leave for 10 minutes. Then mix all the ingredients together to form a firm dough. Knead well. Put the bowl containing the dough in a large polythene bag and leave to rise in a warm place, until the dough has doubled in size. Divide the risen dough in half, knead lightly and put each piece in a greased 2-lb. loaf tin. Cover lightly and leave in a warm place until the dough reaches the tops of the tins. Bake in the centre of a preheated moderate oven (350°F, 180°C, Gas Mark 4) for 40–45 minutes. Turn out onto a wire tray and while hot brush the tops with a glaze made by dissolving the sugar in the milk and boiling it for 1–2 minutes to form a sticky consistency.

Granny's nutty-slack

Mrs. J. M. Harrison, Ramper Farm,
Skegness, Lincs

3 oz. butter
1½ oz. castor sugar
3 oz. golden syrup
4 oz. rolled oats
pinch salt
1½ oz. peanuts, chopped

Makes 8 pieces

Place the butter in a saucepan and melt over a gentle heat. Remove from the heat and stir in sugar, golden syrup, rolled oats, salt (omit the salt if using salted peanuts) and chopped nuts. Spoon into a greased 8-inch sandwich tin and smooth the surface. Bake in the centre of a preheated moderate oven (325°F, 170°C, Gas Mark 3) for 25–30 minutes, until pale brown. Cool slightly and cut into eight pieces; leave to cool completely in the tin.

Note If liked the mixture can be baked in a 7-inch square cake tin and cut into 12 fingers.

Ruddy's breaks (*below*)

Mrs. F. M. Rudd, Littleham House Cottage,
Douglas Avenue, Exmouth, Devon

6 oz. butter
4 oz. sugar
2 tablespoons golden syrup
2 tablespoons clear honey
2 egg yolks
12 oz. plain flour
pinch salt
2 teaspoons mixed spice
2 teaspoons ground ginger
2 teaspoons bicarbonate of soda
chopped nuts to sprinkle

Makes 30–35

Cream the butter and sugar together until light and fluffy. Gently heat the syrup and honey together, cool slightly and beat into the creamed mixture with the egg yolks. Add the flour, salt, mixed spice, ground ginger and bicarbonate of soda and knead the mixture to form a dough. Chill in the refrigerator for 1–2 hours, then roll out on a floured board and cut into various shapes – rounds, squares etc. Place on baking trays, brush the tops with lightly beaten egg white and sprinkle with finely chopped nuts. Bake, in batches, in the centre of a preheated cool oven (300°F, 150°C, Gas Mark 2) for 8–10 minutes. Cool on a wire tray.

Brecon light cakes

Mrs. E. M. Morgan, Lower Cwmclyn,
Libanus, Brecon

2 eggs
juice of 1 orange
4 oz. self-raising flour
pinch salt
2 oz. castor sugar
4–5 tablespoons soured cream
or milk
lard for frying
1 oz. soft brown sugar

Makes 14–16

Beat the eggs with half the orange juice. Sieve the flour and salt into a bowl; stir in the sugar and beaten egg mixture. Add enough soured cream or milk to make a fairly thin batter. Beat thoroughly. Melt a small quantity of lard in a frying pan and pour in small amounts of the batter to make 2–3-inch rounds. When light brown, turn and lightly brown the other side. Drain on absorbent paper; sprinkle with the remaining orange juice and with the soft brown sugar. Serve these cakes on the same day as they are made.